THE POWER *of* OBSERVATION

SECOND EDITION

Judy R. Jablon
Amy Laura Dombro
Margo L. Dichtelmiller

Foreword by Diane Trister Dodge

Published by:
Teaching Strategies, Inc.
P.O. Box 42243
Washington, DC 20015
www.TeachingStrategies.com

National Association for the Education of Young Children
1313 L Street NW, Suite 500
Washington, DC 20005-4101
www.naeyc.org
NAEYC Item #2006

Editors: Hilary Parrish, Laurie Taub, and Nancy Guadagno
Design: Elia Seba
Layout/Production: Jennifer Andruzzi
Illustrations: Jennifer Barrett O'Connell

Copyright © 1999, 2007
by Judy R. Jablon, Amy Laura Dombro, and Margo L. Dichtelmiller

First edition 1999
Second edition 2007

ISBN: 978-1-933021-52-2

Library of Congress Cataloging-in-Publication Data

Jablon, Judy R.

  The power of observation / Judy R. Jablon, Amy Laura Dombro, Margo L. Dichtelmiller ; foreword
by Diane Trister Dodge. -- 2nd ed.

     p. cm.

  Includes bibliographical references.

  ISBN 978-1-933021-52-2

  1. Observation (Educational method) 2. Child development. I. Dombro, Amy Laura, 1953- II.
Dichtelmiller, Margo L. (Margo Lizabeth), 1954- III. Title.

  LB1027.28.J33 2007

  370.71'1--dc22

                         2007013314

Table of Contents

Acknowledgments

T he *Power of Observation* is based on our experiences as caregivers and teachers and on the ideas and experiences of many educators with whom we have worked and to whom we owe tremendous appreciation.

A special thanks goes to Chayim Dimont, Marilyn Dolbeare-Mathews, Erlene Ellis, Amy-Beth Fischoff, Gail Gordon, and Barb Prevost, who worked with us intensively for a year, providing observations of children with whom they work, answering our questions, and reflecting aloud about their personal experiences as observers. Their stories are the primary source of the examples and reflections included here.

Each of us has worked extensively with programs and individuals across the country whose questions, insights, challenges, and lessons learned about observation inspired us to write *The Power of Observation* and informed our choice of ideas to include. To the following individuals and programs we extend our appreciation: the Early Learning Branch of the Maryland Department of Education and the teachers and assistants involved in the Maryland Model for School Readiness; Heather Charles and Traci Jones of Crystal Lakes Elementary School, West Palm Beach, Florida; the staff of Gamma House in Camden, New Jersey; Mary Cunningham-DeLuca, Brenda Davis, and Shelley Hawver of Community Action Agency Head Start and Early Head Start, Jackson, Michigan; Learning Readiness and Early Childhood Family Education programs, Minnesota; Betty Cook and the Minnesota Department of Children, Families, and Learning; Melissa Shamblott, Renie Willard, and Gail Roberts of the St. Paul Public Schools, Minnesota, and Jonathan Fribley, St. Cloud Public Schools, St. Cloud, Minnesota.

Amanda Napolitani, Wendy Arnold, Ann Cramer, and many other early childhood teachers from New Jersey offered stories and insights that enriched the second edition. Thank you.

As we worked on this revision, Holly Seplocha offered guidance on chapter 6. Charlotte Stetson assisted with the list of resources. Thank you both.

We extend appreciation to Samuel J. Meisels for his encouragement at the outset of this project. To Dorothea Marsden and Charlotte Stetson, special thanks for their willingness to read early drafts of the manuscript and get us on the right track. Thanks to Jim Levine for answering our many questions and providing excellent advice and direction.

We thank everyone at Teaching Strategies for their confidence and support. Diane's skill at clarifying ideas amazes us, and we thank her for the support she provided in shaping the final manuscript. Thanks to Larry Bram for coming up with our title and for getting *The Power of Observation* into the early childhood community. To Hilary Parrish, Laurie Taub, and Nancy Guadagno, our editors; to Elia Seba for his beautiful design concept; and to Jennifer Andruzzi for her layout and careful design work, thanks for transforming our manuscript into a book.

We hope our book will show readers the close link among observation, building relationships with children and families, and effective caregiving and teaching.

Judy R. Jablon
Amy Laura Dombro
Margo L. Dichtelmiller
May 2007

Foreword to the Second Edition

This book greatly expanded my understanding of how powerful the observation of children can be. Because it has the potential truly to transform the daily life and effectiveness of early childhood educators, helping teachers observe with intention is a very important emphasis in our work at Teaching Strategies.

We decided to publish *The Power of Observation* because there is a strong link between observing young children and implementing a curriculum effectively. The authors are especially qualified to inspire and guide teachers in understanding this link. They have many years of experience in working with young children and providing staff development on observation. As thoughtful educators and authors, they listened respectfully to the stories of other teachers and used what they learned to write this book.

All of us share the common goal of strengthening the quality of early childhood programs. Teaching Strategies focuses on developing curriculum, assessment, and professional development resources, so we know that support and training are essential if teachers are to understand and use a curriculum to guide their everyday decision making. Effective curriculum implementation requires a good understanding of child development and of each child's unique abilities, interests, and needs. When teachers and family child care providers observe children systematically, they have a wealth of information for implementing curriculum and individualizing instruction.

The care and education of young children is important and challenging work. Our profession is deeply satisfying because of the relationships we form with each child and family, not just the children who are easy to reach and the families that are eager to be partners. There are always children who seem to get lost in a group, whose behavior perplexes us, and whose strengths are not immediately obvious to us. Some family situations make it more difficult to forge partnerships. We must not lose these children and families, and observation provides much of the information that we need to have in order to build positive relationships. We also owe it to ourselves to be successful and satisfied rather than frustrated and ineffective in our work. This book is important because thoughtful observation enhances our relationships.

I urge you to think about your own experiences with young children as you read *The Power of Observation*. Which children get your attention each day? Which children mystify you? Think of a child you were not sure you could reach until you made the effort really to get to know and appreciate that child's unique qualities. Knowing children as individuals—their interests, their interpretations of experiences, their best ways of learning, their special skills and abilities—enables us to tailor our practices to help every child succeed.

Observation also helps build relationships with families. As an experienced teacher and trainer, Elizabeth Servidio, once said to me, "It's very hard for parents not to like a teacher who really appreciates and likes their child." This book shows us how observation reveals what is unique and special about each child—even a child whose behavior challenges and frustrates us—and how this knowledge empowers us to partner with families. It acknowledges the very real barriers to observation and offers creative and practical strategies for addressing them.

This second edition of *The Power of Observation* is different from the first in several ways. Chapter 6 now includes an overview of the observation cycle and more stories that show how teachers use what they learn by observing. Some of the stories illustrate specific points about making your program responsive to individual children and the group and about working together with families. Others will help you think about the various phases of the observation cycle. The consistent feature of the stories is that they show how observation strengthens relationships and promotes children's success as learners.

A short discussion of research about relationships has been added to chapter 1, and the resource list has also been updated. In response to readers' requests, a study guide has been added as Appendix A. It can be used to support professional development in a variety of settings and as a knowledge check for all readers. Answers to frequently asked questions have been reorganized as Appendix B.

The Power of Observation makes a major contribution to the early childhood field because skilled observation supports teachers in implementing an appropriate curriculum. We are delighted that NAEYC has chosen this book as a comprehensive membership benefit, thereby making it available to a wider audience.

Diane Trister Dodge
President
Teaching Strategies, Inc.

Introduction

The *Power of Observation* is a personal, reflective look at observing. In this book, we invite you to join us in exploring the vital connection between observing and your day-to-day work with children and families.

We define observation as watching to learn. Observing provides the information you need to build relationships with individual children and enable them to be successful learners. We learn about children by carefully watching them, listening to them, and studying their work. Watching and listening to children helps us understand what they are feeling, learning, and thinking.

Getting to know children as people and as learners gives you the information you need to be an effective decision maker in the classroom. With the information you learn from observing, you can select the right materials, plan appropriate activities, and ask questions that guide children in learning to understand the world around them.

Each child has a unique way of approaching learning. For example, one child may be an active explorer, intensely curious and imaginative. Another might be quiet, taking time to look around before getting involved in play or work. Every child is intrigued by something that ignites her wonder and provides insight into the essence of that child as a person and a learner. It may be music, frogs, penguins, painting, building with blocks, or something you can't yet imagine. As you watch, listen, and interact with children to discover their interests and approaches to learning, meaningful relationships develop.

The relationships that develop as you get to know and interact with children and family members affect everything that happens in your setting. When children and adults are recognized and respected, they feel good about themselves. When they feel a connection with you, they feel safe to explore, experiment, question, and test new limits—all prerequisites for learning. For all teachers, the key to effectiveness is trusting and responsive relationships. And observation is key to building these relationships.

A Personal Look at Observation

Like you, we have each worked with children and families and experienced our own successes and struggles with observing. In this book, we share our experiences and those of many other caregivers and teachers, inviting you to think with us about how observing already works for you, and about how to refine your observation skills and transform observing into an even more useful tool.

Here are some personal experiences that convinced us that observation and good teaching go hand-in-hand:

Amy: Johnny was a red-headed 2-year-old who could empty a shelf of toys faster than any child I've ever known. I would spend the days he came to child care racing around after him, trying to keep some semblance of order. Around this time, I had to take a course on observing as part of my studies at Bank Street. I was upset. I knew how to watch children. I could see what they were doing. After about 2 months, it dawned on me: Observing wasn't just about what children do. It was watching them from the outside with the purpose of trying to understand what they are feeling and experiencing on the inside. This revelation helped me get to know Johnny. I began using observing to help me look at the world through his eyes and was surprised to see that he was bright, curious, and had a sense of humor. I noticed he loved music and would spend up to 5 to 10 minutes at a time strumming on a toy guitar. This was a far cry from my original opinion of him as chaotic. As I began sitting and singing with him and bringing out other instruments, something changed. I'm embarrassed to admit it, but one of those things was that I began liking him. He had to sense it because he started spending more time with me reading, talking, and preparing snack and less time scattering toys around. Our relationship, born out of observing, centered him and gave us the means to enjoy and learn from one another.

Margo: Tony, a 4-year-old, came to my special education preschool with a great deal of advance notice. Many people on my classroom team had visited his home, a mobile home in a trailer park, and interviewed his parents, two very warm people who were mildly mentally retarded. My team members described Tony's somewhat unusual appearance: short for his age, large head, short arms, big glasses, and a very nasal voice. And they made long lists of objectives for Tony to work on in my classroom.

When it was time for Tony to start school, I felt a little apprehensive because he had been described as "very active" at home. Based on all I had heard, I was expecting a child who struggled to learn and who would have a hard time adjusting to the order and routine of my classroom. Instead, I observed a very alert and curious child. True, he looked and sounded a little different. But as I watched him those first weeks of school, I realized he moved from one thing to another so quickly because everything was new to him. Although he was interested in other children and tried to approach them, he didn't know how to make friends. But Tony learned the rules and routines of the classroom within the first week. He began picking up on pre-academic skills almost immediately, and his language skills improved dramatically within the first 2 months. Although he had difficulty with gross and fine motor skills, they too improved with practice.

As I look back, I marvel about how destructive it would have been if I had let my preconceived ideas about Tony influence how I saw him in my classroom. When I began to talk about his eagerness to learn and the rapid pace of his learning to my team members, they had a hard time believing it, but I kept encouraging them to come and watch him in the classroom.

Judy: It was my second year of teaching, and I struggled to find a way to connect with Rachel, a third grader in my classroom. But, no matter what I tried, we just didn't click. My observations of her continually reaffirmed my first impressions—she was unresponsive to activities, defying directions, and provoking her peers (and me). To be honest, I looked forward to the days she was absent.

Mid-year, a student teacher, Lisa, came to work in my classroom. From the minute she arrived, I was aware of her competence with the children and what an asset she would be. The afternoon of her second day, the children were working in small groups on different projects related to our study of the Hopi. Lisa joined a group of children who were painting a mural of the desert. Rachel was in this group. Although I was busy with other groups, I periodically glanced over to see how Rachel's group was doing. At one point I noticed Rachel rush to the bookshelves to find a book with a picture of a cactus. Later I saw the group laughing together.

After school I asked Lisa to tell me about her work with the group, but I said nothing about Rachel. Lisa had many observations about individual students. She commented on Rachel's enthusiasm and her sense of humor, but said nothing about her negativity. I told her about my experiences with Rachel. The next day I greeted Rachel by letting her know that Lisa had told me what a great sense of humor she had. Rachel smiled, said thanks, and rushed off to put her backpack away. All day I worked at seeing Rachel through Lisa's eyes, trying to set aside my feelings about her. I did notice many new things about Rachel that I just couldn't see before. In the first few days after Lisa came, Rachel and I had more positive interactions than we'd had all year. Lisa's arrival in my classroom had a big impact on me. I learned the value of seeking another perspective about a child when my own feelings were so strong.

In addition to our personal experiences as teachers, our experiences as staff developers confirmed to us the power of observation. As we work with teachers to improve their observation skills, or as they learn to use observational assessments, we find that some of them easily grasp how observing can help them and quickly incorporate it into their classroom routine. They constantly share how much more they know about their students. Others have more of a struggle. The teachers who struggle have pushed us to reflect more on our own experiences with observing and puzzle over how to make observing more accessible.

Gradually, as some of these teachers caught on, they began to interact with children in different ways, and became more excited about their work. We realized that too often teachers overfocus on the "how to" of observing. They get stuck trying to design the perfect record keeping system and worrying about whether they are doing it "right," and never get to the point when observing benefits their relationships and their work with children. Listening to the stories of teachers has helped us appreciate the role observing plays in supporting children's learning and eliciting effective caregiving and teaching.

Beyond a Set of Skills: Observing As an Attitude of Openness

If we all agree that observing is important, why is it so often a hit-or-miss affair and a source of great frustration? "I can go for months without giving observation a thought," one teacher told us. "I set out with good intentions," explains another. "Then at the end of the year, I find a pile of index cards in the drawer that I never looked at. It's frustrating."

We understand. We've been there. In the years since we left our teaching positions to develop educational materials and conduct staff development workshops, we have talked with hundreds of teachers with similar stories. Some of these conversations have occurred in one-on-one interviews, some during classroom visits, and others during workshops. A clear pattern has emerged: Teachers know observing is important. But most don't see themselves as effective observers and, thus, feel unable to reap the full benefits of observing.

Why does this gap exist? We believe the answer lies in how we have been taught to think about observing. Many of us were taught a set of skills, including looking at children's behavior, objectively recording what we see, and then analyzing our notes. Observing is all of these things, but it is so much more.

We believe that observing creates an attitude of openness and wonder that allows you to know and understand the children you work with every day. Observing is essential to building the trusting relationships with children and families that provide the foundation for a successful early childhood program. Only within the context of these trusting relationships can teachers promote children's development. Observing is so much more than a set of skills or another task to add to your already demanding schedule.

Getting to know a child is not a static process, though we each tend to form initial impressions—"She's quiet" or "He's trouble"—and often get stuck there. One teacher told us this about a quiet child: "I thought she was shy and hesitant until I began observing. Then I realized she was quiet, yes, but she was a leader and a risk-taker." Observing can help you go beyond your expectations or assumptions to see the many dimensions of a child that are revealed over time.

This subtle shift from seeing observation as a skill to seeing it as an opportunity to wonder and learn makes an enormous difference. Suddenly, observation is no longer something "out there" that you have to find time to do. Instead, it becomes part of your everyday work. Wondering and asking; watching, listening, and taking notes; and reflecting and responding are as important as anything else you do during the day. They also have implications for the way you see your role as a teacher.

For some teachers, this shift is jarring. "When I observe, I'm just standing there. But I'm a teacher. I'm supposed to teach," explained a first-grade teacher at a recent observation workshop. "How am I supposed to do both?" he asked. Our answer: It isn't a question of either-or. Teaching well and observation are one.

For others, it takes time to adjust. A second-grade teacher told us: "For me, observing regularly meant an attitude shift. But after I did it for awhile, it became part of who I am as a teacher."

> *What are the implications of this shift for you?*
> *How does it affect your sense of self as a teacher?*
> *How does it affect your sense of self as an observer?*

What Lies Ahead

Many excellent books and videos on observing children's learning include information about child development and what to look for at different ages. This is not one of them. In *The Power of Observation*, we discuss the practice of observation and how to be a more effective observer. However, unlike other books about observing, our focus is on you, not the child.

Chapter 2 describes the power of observation as the way to get to know, respect, and appreciate children—the basis for building trusting, responsive relationships with them. These relationships are the foundation of effective caregiving and teaching.

In chapter 3, we invite you to think about what you bring to your role as observer and how you can use this self-awareness to be as objective as possible.

In chapters 4 and 5, we turn to the practice of observing. In chapter 4 you will find guidelines for effective observation. Chapter 5 takes a close look at the day-to-day decisions you make while observing and offers practical suggestions for observing in your setting.

Chapter 6 highlights ways to use what you learn by observing to make your program responsive to children, to respond to individuals and the group, to assess and report, and to work together with families. Chapter 7 offers strategies for getting started.

Appendix A is "The Power of Learning With Others: A Study Guide." It includes discussion questions and exercises to use in promoting professional development and collaboration in child care and school settings and through college courses. Appendix B offers answers to frequently asked questions.

You may be a new caregiver or teacher or an experienced veteran. You may care for infants and toddlers or teach third graders. You may work in a child care center, family child care home, preschool, Head Start program, or school. Regardless of the setting or the age group you teach, you—and all the other early childhood teachers we know—care deeply about children and want to do a good job. Every day you work hard to help children and their family members feel connected and competent. You promote their learning by offering an environment and experiences that invite them to explore, discover, and construct meaning. It isn't always easy, and yet you persevere.

Observation can play an important role. The more you observe, the better you will know children and how to promote their success as learners. Their success, in turn, will help you feel successful, and the cycle will continue. Your challenge is to make meaning from your observations and take full advantage of the wealth of insights observation offers you day in and day out. *The Power of Observation* can help.

Using Observation to Build Relationships

When you observe, you slow down, listen more carefully, and pause to reflect before stepping in to offer direction or help. You see and respond to who a child is and what a child needs. Observing helps you build relationships by revealing the uniqueness of every child—including the child's temperament, strengths, personality, work style, and preferred mode of expression.

Positive relationships between children and teachers are the foundation for children's exploration of and learning within the classroom (Howes & Ritchie, 2002). As children develop trust in their teachers, they become more likely to take on new challenges, continue trying, and ask questions when confused. All of these behaviors enhance learning (Stipek, 2006). Positive relationships with teachers lead to more engaged learners and higher levels of achievement (Osterman, 2000; Pianta, 1999).

What are these relationships like? They are warm, sensitive, and nurturing. Effective caregivers and teachers observe children and think carefully about what children do and say. They know and respond to children as individuals. They listen to children, are dependable, guide children's behavior in positive ways, maintain high expectations, and join children in their play and learning (Howes & Ritchie, 2002; Shonkoff & Phillips, 2000; Stipek, 2006).

Many teachers have shared with us how today's emphasis on outcomes distracts them from building positive relationships with children. However, building trusting, responsive relationships with children is not just another chore for already overworked teachers. It is the essence of good teaching and requires a willingness to become a learner and to wonder and ask questions about children. That wondering and questioning is the first step in the ongoing cycle of observation.

Here is what some caregivers and teachers have to say about how observing has influenced their way of being with children and their relationships with them:

> It is the act of observing—of giving someone my attention and trying to understand that child—that opens my heart. As I observe, I begin to get to know a child. A feeling bridge is built. The details I observe start to come together, and I begin to see what the child needs from me.

> Observing slows me down. I listen to children more. I engage with them instead of teaching at them.

> I use observation to get to know children better—to figure out how to relate to them better and to teach them better. By observing, I know that Thalia has a sense of humor because I have seen that little smile and the twinkle in her eye. I'm going to figure out ways to get that twinkle in her eye a little more often.

> *Reflect on a child you know well. How would you describe your relationship with the child? How did your relationship begin? What made you start feeling connected to the child? How did it feel? What role did observing play?*

Observing fosters your relationships with children by helping you do three important things:

- Get to know children.

- Respect and appreciate children.

- Intervene in ways that enable children to be successful learners.

Getting to Know Each Child

Think about the children you work with each day. Write down each child's name. Next to each name write down the child's age and something you have observed about that child.

Alex (6 mos):	*Babbles back when I talk with him*
Maria (26 mos):	*Cries a lot lately when her grandmother leaves in the morning*
Tony (3 yrs):	*Sits and watches every morning before joining in*
Baili (3 yrs):	*Told me about making dumplings with her parents over the weekend*
Katy (5 yrs):	*Drew a picture of Iris, her cat*
William (5 yrs):	*Built a barn with stalls and a milking machine*
Denise (7 yrs):	*Counted out coins for another child's change at our classroom bookstore*
Alexander (7 yrs):	*Reading his third book about whales*

Now it's your turn. On a sheet of paper, list your observations.

> *How did it go? Were you surprised to find that you couldn't think of something to write about some children? Did you forget to put some children on your list, children who have been invisible to you?*

You most likely found that you know some children better than others. Most teachers do. Who are these children? Teachers we have talked with say they know most about the children they feel connected to in some way. These are usually children whose personalities, behavior, and/or family's values strike a familiar chord in the teacher.

Teachers also seem to know those children who by themselves or with family members create a big presence. Ironically, sometimes the personalities, strengths, and needs of these children are blurred by teachers' own experiences, assumptions, and prejudices. We'll talk more about this in the next chapter.

There is always something new to learn about a child—even a child you think you know well. Try to make a habit of asking questions (or acknowledging your questions). This will help you get to know a child and who that child is becoming over time.

Questions to Help You Get to Know Children

What are some of your questions about the children with whom you work? Observing can help you learn about a child's:

- **Health and physical development.** How would you generally describe the child's health? What do the child's health records reveal? Have family members raised any questions or concerns about a child's health or development? Have any occurred to you?

- **Temperament.**[1] Can a child generally be described as flexible? Slow-to-warm or fearful? Feisty or intense? Though children don't fall into neat categories, having a sense of a child's temperament may help you to predict and understand that child's behavior.

---

[1] Infant researchers Stella Chess and Alexander Thomas (1996) have identified three basic types of temperaments. The Program for Infant/Toddler Caregivers, developed by West Laboratory for Educational Research and Development in collaboration with the California Department of Education, has named these flexible, fearful, and feisty (Lally, Mangione, & Signer, 1990).

- **Skills and abilities.** What does the child do well? What does the child find challenging? What skills is the child currently working on?

- **Interests.** What topics cause a child's eyes to light up? What does the child talk about? What does the child do when given the opportunity to choose?

- **Culture and home life.** What do you know about the child's culture and life at home? For example: Who are the members of the child's family? What language is spoken in the child's home? Do family members play different roles in child rearing? How is discipline handled?

- **Approach to learning.** How does the child approach new material? How does the child interact with materials? What is the child's preferred way of expressing himself or herself?

- **Use of verbal language.** Does the child speak? If so, how much language does he or she have? With whom does the child talk? Other children? Other adults? What kinds of things does the child talk about? Is the child comfortable speaking one-on-one? In a group?

- **Use of body language.** How does the child move? Does the child use gestures? Is the child physically expressive?

- **Social interactions with adults and peers.** Does the child seem comfortable interacting with adults? Other children? Familiar people? New people? How does the child initiate interactions? What kinds of activities does the child do with others? How does the child handle conflicts with others? In what situations does the child seek adult help?

Observing to Find Answers

Specific questions give you a focus for your observations and help you find answers. Over time, you have repeated opportunities to witness children practicing skills, demonstrating knowledge, and exhibiting behaviors in a familiar and comfortable environment. You can observe not only what children know, but also how they think and solve problems. By collecting observations over time, you find the answers to your questions and build a picture of children's performance and progress without interfering in any way with their daily activities or "natural" behavior.

For example, when Laura, an infant caregiver, senses something amiss with 5-month-old Kara's fine motor development, she goes to the observational checklist she uses regularly to monitor children's fine and gross motor development. Based on her observations, she realizes Kara isn't bringing both hands to midline, while Taylor, who is the same age, does so frequently. Laura plans to continue observing. She will talk to the physical therapist who consults with the program about ways to help Kara reach this milestone.

Kathy's teacher photographed the castle she constructed in the block area. Another day, he quickly sketched the pattern block design Kathy, age 4, made in the math center. On yet a third occasion, he saved a collage Kathy made. When it comes time to evaluate Kathy's performance and progress, his judgments about her sense of balance and symmetry will be based on these and many other observations.

A third-grade teacher monitors Brendon's developing spelling skills by observing him as he writes and studying his written work. Here are the brief notes she recorded at three different times.

3/12
Conference w/me, B self-corrected 3 words.

3/24
Taking more chances writing "hard words" (Atlatik Osen—Atlantic Ocean).

4/20
Using word cards to help w/science writing.

These collected observations enable her to evaluate Brendon's spelling. They provide specific examples of Brendon's behavior and accomplishments to share with his parents at their upcoming conference. And they provide data she needs to determine how to intervene in ways that help Brendon continue to see himself as a successful learner.

Getting to know children by asking questions and assessing their learning is one step in building a relationship, but there are more. Engaging in a relationship with children also involves finding something you respect and appreciate about each child—something that draws you in and makes you invested in that child's well-being and success.

Respecting and Appreciating Children

Think about a friend who accepts you as you are and takes pleasure in your accomplishments. How do you feel when you are with this person? At ease? Competent? Confident? Acknowledged for who you are? Trusting? Proud? Supported? Secure? Willing to take risks?

These feelings are the building blocks of self-confidence that we want all children to experience. How the children in your group feel about themselves depends in large part on how you respond to their actions, ideas, questions, and work. And how they feel about themselves will influence how they feel about and interact with others. As children come to see that you respect their work, their discoveries, and their ideas, they will come to respect themselves.

Sometimes your respect and appreciation for children blossoms as your picture of them becomes clearer. Often, this also strengthens your relationship. You can convey your respect and appreciation to children in many ways; here are just a few:

- Listen and respond to children's sounds, facial expressions, gestures, words, and body language.

- Show children you care about what they do and say. Comment on what you see them doing. Then pause and wait for their response (e.g., say, "Your building is really tall," then pause for a response. Or, after watching for several minutes, comment, "I notice that when you poured water through the top of the water wheel, the wheel began turning around").

- Ask open-ended questions that invite many responses and let them know that there is no right or wrong answer (e.g., What do you think might happen next in the story? What do you remember about our trip to the fire station? Why do you think Clifford did that?).

- Demonstrate your recognition of children's competence by providing opportunities for them to help and teach one another. And don't hesitate to ask children a question or for some help.

- Show children that you have time to listen and be with them. Sit down with a child instead of talking on the run. Don't let interruptions by other children distract your time with a child. Explain that you are busy and will see them when you are finished.

There will be instances, of course, when a child pushes one of your buttons or rubs you the wrong way. It can be uncomfortable to admit you have negative feelings about a child, and all too often teachers tend to keep them a secret. If you acknowledge these feelings to yourself and/or a trusted colleague, it will help you get a handle on them and avoid letting them color your daily interactions. How you respond to children shapes how children see themselves and interact with others. Thus, how you feel about them is as important as what you say or do together.

The Powerful Influence of Your Feelings About Children

Children have an uncanny ability to tune into how you feel about them. They sense your feelings in the way you hold them, the expression on your face, and your tone of voice.

Because you play such an important role in their lives, they care about how you feel and they want your approval. Like the ripples caused when you throw a stone into a pond, your feelings about individual children have a far-reaching influence that touches children's developing sense of self, their impressions of and interactions with one another, and even how their parents view you and them. Here is what three teachers have observed about the impact of their feelings:

> Christiane cried inconsolably after her mother left in the morning. Her crying was so intense it frightened me. I would hold her, hoping the crying would stop—but it didn't. One day I realized it was all right that she was upset and that I could help her. I held her as usual, the only difference being my sense of confidence that she would be OK. She cried as usual, but by the next day, her sobs began turning to sniffles after only a few minutes. It's amazing— the power of your feelings—isn't it?

◆　　◆　　◆　　◆　　◆　　◆

As I build relationships with kids, they know I am interested in them. They relax with me, and I'm more relaxed too. They tell me wonderful stories and jokes. We laugh a lot. When the room is more relaxed, I'm more willing to set up cooperative active learning experiences that the kids enjoy and learn from.

When Sarah first came into my class, I tiptoed around her—and her mother. They both had a reputation for being difficult, and I wanted to avoid a scene. I recently told Sarah's mom, "I really like your daughter." She cried because no one had ever said that to her before. I told her that her daughter is a good worker and cooperates with other children. Funny thing is, at first, I had assumed Sarah was a problem, and I used to jump to the conclusion that when there was a dispute among a group, she was the cause. Observing helped me see her for who she is and appreciate her—and helped me forge an alliance with her mom.

But what about those children—and there are always some—whom you find unappealing or annoying and, to be honest, shy away from? We know you want to give your best to all children—but some children require more effort than others. The first step is to look beyond a child's drooling, crying, constant activity, shyness, troublemaking, or whatever other aspect of behavior you find off-putting. The next step is to find a point of connection.

Connecting With Children

Remember Amy's story about Johnny? Her discomfort in dealing with this active toddler could have made her constantly restrict his behavior. Put yourself in Johnny's place for a moment. How would this have made you feel about yourself? Instead, through observing, Amy came to see him as a unique individual and to appreciate his zest for life and sense of humor. This doesn't mean she never said no or set limits on his behavior. But her interactions were colored by her respect and newfound delight in him. As a result, Johnny was helped to feel good about himself as an explorer rather than seeing himself as someone thwarted at every turn.

Do you have a Johnny in your group? Can you use observation to find a point of entry into a relationship with this child by asking yourself such questions as:

- What issues is the child dealing with?
- In what situations does the child seem most comfortable?
- What causes the child's eyes to brighten, what brings a smile?
- What does the child do well?
- What does the child talk, read, or write about?
- What does the child paint, build, or draw?
- What are the main themes of the child's dramatic play?
- Is there an adult, child, or activity that seems to draw the child out?

Sometimes the answers are evident—once you take the time to stop and look. When you observe that Carlos talks constantly about his new baby brother and spends all his time in dramatic play wanting to be a baby, you have a clue about how to approach him and insight into why he's been so clingy and whiny lately. Discovering during recess that Ralene, so annoying during group time, is a terrific climber and that she runs with great coordination and enthusiasm leads you to tell her that you have noticed her wonderful outdoor skills. Her pleasure in your validation results in several positive interactions, and you begin to see her in a new light. Although her behavior at group time may not look different, you feel differently about it. Your change in attitude toward her may have a positive influence on her. Or you may incorporate her observed strength into a group time conversation. Asking children to describe their favorite things to do outside might provide Ralene with a way to make a meaningful contribution and give her a positive experience during a routine that is typically hard for her. Her feeling of success in this situation is likely to lead to other successes.

Sometimes answers are not as apparent. Indeed, you may not even know where to begin looking. You realize you do not know enough, so you go back to the beginning—getting to know a child.

Other times discovering a point of contact with a child may require some flexibility and openness on your part. Getting to know the child who delights in the frogs she discovers during a class trip to a nearby pond may mean that you have to move beyond your negative attitude toward amphibians. When you learn that a child you assumed to be a natural troublemaker knows a lot about the space shuttle program, your plans for creating a store in the dramatic play area may end up being set aside—at least temporarily—to make room for a refrigerator-box space capsule and mission control center.

Fostering Children's Competence and Success

Observing gives you the information you need to make decisions about when and how to intervene with children. You want your actions to help children see themselves as successful learners and, at the same time, strengthen your relationships with them. You can use the information you learn from observing to create your classroom's physical and social environment and to plan your daily routines and activities. The environment you create leads children to certain kinds of discoveries and thinking and to the acquisition of certain skills. Your role is to facilitate children's thinking and learning as they discover their own meaning of their experiences.

Too often, however, teachers intervene in ways that are oriented toward an activity, not toward children and their learning. Think, for example, about the infant teacher who takes babies' hands in hers to glue cut-out umbrellas to a collage for her "Spring Showers" bulletin board. Or the second-grade teacher who brings out the unifix cubes and persists in conducting a lesson on fractions when children clearly are fascinated by creating symmetrical patterns. Interventions such as these lead to frustration instead of learning.

As you get to know children, and your respect and appreciation for them grows, your decisions about how and when to intervene will more likely be based on children's interests and needs. This is the essence of individualizing.

Ask yourself three basic questions before intervening:

1. Should I step back and give children the space and time they need to make a discovery or solve a problem independently?

2. Does the child need me to step in and help?

3. If I step in, what should I say or do?

Sometimes the best thing you can do to support a child's learning is to step back and let the child experience something. Taking a few moments to observe a child at play or work may be just what you need to figure out if you should stay out of the action. When you do step in, rely on your observations to ask the right questions to stimulate and stretch the child's thinking.

Often you don't have to say much. A simple comment or question, such as, "Tell me how you decided to use the colors on your painting that way" or "I noticed that you seem to be putting the unifix cubes in a special order. Do you have a rule?" can do the trick. Our colleague Diane Trister Dodge tells a great story about a 4-year-old who was sorting a group of objects. The child put a pig and a cup in the same group. At first, his teacher started to intervene. But then she asked, "Tell me about your plan for sorting. How did you decide what things to put in the same group?" The little boy responded, "Well, I'm not really sure if a pig gives milk, but if it does, it needs a cup to put it in."

Here are some examples of how observing can help you decide what to do:

- **Step in and make a suggestion.** You notice that each time a child sets a square block on top of the cylinder the blocks topple. You could help or you could wait to see what happens. Watching lets you learn about the child's problem-solving skills. If after awhile, you sense she is frustrated, you might step in and comment, "I see that you have tried putting the square on the top of the cylinder and it keeps toppling. Why do you think that is happening?" Then wait and see what she says or does.

She may have only needed you to describe what she was doing to come up with another idea. Or, she may need you to suggest that she try putting a larger block on the bottom. If that works, you may ask, "Why do you think it is not falling over?" By giving her time to experiment and then being there to offer support when she needs it, you have encouraged her to use trial and error—a basic problem-solving strategy—and provided her with helpful language—cylinder, square, balance, top, bottom—for thinking about the problem.

- **Wait and watch.** Imagine you have just come back from a walk and you notice an infant is trying to pull off his hat. Should you step back or take action? You observe and see that he looks engaged and determined as he pulls on it. You decide to step back and keep your eye on him. Two minutes later, he is smiling, the hat in hand. If he had started getting upset or frustrated, if the hat got stuck and was covering his eyes or nose, you would have intervened in a different way.

- **Describe a child's actions.** You see a preschool child who is struggling to fit LEGO® pieces together. You wait and watch. She tries several different pieces and finally comes up with a solution. She cries out, "Finally!" You respond with, "I noticed you tried many different pieces until you got one to fit. That was good work."

- **Use prior knowledge to prevent a conflict.** Imagine two first graders struggling over one bottle of glue. What you know from prior observation will help you decide what to do. Because one child has been hitting lately, you might step in and offer a cup of glue with two popsicle sticks, a second bottle of glue, or simply hand the glue bottle to one child and say to the other, "I know it is hard to wait but it will be your turn in a minute." By intervening, you aid both children, and the child who has been hitting learns how it feels to resolve a conflict without hurting another child.

- **Use observations to foster competence and success.** Think back to the children we talked about at the beginning of this chapter. In the chart that follows, you'll see decisions we might make to promote their learning based on our knowledge, appreciation, and respect for them. The next time you observe, think about how something you see influences how you intervene to support a child's success.

CHILD'S NAME/AGE	WHAT WE OBSERVED	WHAT WE MIGHT DO
Alex (6 months)	*Babbles back when you talk with him*	• Promote his language development by talking about what you are doing as you feed, change, and dress him. Give him time to respond with sounds and gestures.
Maria (22 months)	*Cries lately when her grandmother leaves in the morning*	• Be available to support her when it is time for grandmother to say good-bye. • Show respect and let her know she can share her feelings with you by listening to her and acknowledging her feelings. • Show her the picture of her family hanging on the wall.
Tony (3 years)	*Sits and watches every morning before joining in*	• Greet and welcome him when he arrives. Explain what is going on in the room. Give him the time he needs to survey the scene and feel comfortable.
Baili (3 years)	*Told about making dumplings with her parents over the weekend*	• Provide cultural continuity by talking about foods children eat at home. • Add books with pictures of foods from different cultures to the library corner. • Invite Baili's parent(s) to come prepare dumplings or another favorite dish with the children.

CHILD'S NAME/AGE	WHAT WE OBSERVED	WHAT WE MIGHT DO
Katy (5 years)	*Drew a picture of her cat, Iris*	• Help Katy bridge her worlds of home and kindergarten by asking about Iris when you discover a picture of a cat in the book you are reading together.
William (5 years)	*Built a barn complete with stalls and a milking machine in the block area*	• Ask him how he helps his older brother milk the cows in the barn. • Reinforce what he knows by hanging up pictures of the interior and exterior of barns in the block area.
Denise (7 years)	*Counted out coins for another child's change at the classroom bookstore*	• Encourage this new skill by inviting her to help another child count change when it is his turn to be the cashier.
Alexander (7 years)	*Read his third book about whales*	• Build on his interest by suggesting he look for other books and perhaps videos about whales—and maybe other marine mammals—during our next visit to the library. • Invite him to share what he has learned during group time.

We encourage you to step back occasionally and enjoy the children. Everyone will benefit. Your work will be so much more satisfying, your relationships with parents enriched by the stories you share with them, and the children will thrive.

We have been talking about building relationships. In the next chapter, we turn our attention to you—the observer and relationship-builder.

You as Observer

An observation is like a photograph—it captures a moment in time. As an observer, you are like the photographer, focusing on some things, ignoring others. Like the photographer, you bring your own ideas, preferences, and perceptions to the act of observing.

We can never eliminate the personal side of observing, nor would we want to. But we do need to be aware of it because what you bring to observing shapes how you see children and families, which in turn affects your relationships with them.

Have you ever observed a child's behavior and thought, I've seen this a hundred times? Then, before you know it, you find yourself forming an assumption based on one observation: "This child is aggressive" or "This child is shy."

For most of us, the moment we make an assumption, previous experiences or events related to the assumption come to mind. Imagine a computer in your head that, just as you make an assumption, delivers a script describing how to act. You begin interacting with a child according to this script, which influences how the child responds. The first round of a continuing cycle has begun. The potential for getting to know, respect, and appreciate a child for who he or she is gets lost and, with it, the opportunity to support the child's learning in the best way possible.

Why does this happen? Often it happens simply because knowing something is far more comfortable for most of us than not knowing. The more quickly we can get a handle on individual children, the more competent and in control we feel. In addition, people working with young children are often juggling many balls at the same time and have an enormous number of demands on their time. As a result, they tend to do things in a hurry—including forming hasty opinions of children. Let's face it, making snap judgments is human nature. But if we understand this tendency, we can take steps to guard against it.

In this chapter, we invite you to think about what you bring to observing and the steps you can take to make sure that your pictures of children and relationships with them reflect who they actually are rather than who you assume they are.

What You Bring to Observing

Your culture, your individual temperament, interests, feelings, and your professional knowledge and experience color the lens through which you observe. When you are aware of these factors you increase the chances that your observations will give you insight into children, and that your relationships with them will be authentic. Over time you will learn to trust your observations and come to depend on what you bring to help you tune into a child's uniqueness. An infant-toddler teacher describes what this is like for her:

> Observing is about understanding human beings. That's something I try to do in my everyday life. I peer into people and try to get to know them. At work, I may have trouble remembering what a child's coat looks like or whose spoon is whose. But when it comes to a child's temperament and personality, I see things clearly. It is why I went into this work in the first place.

You will also come to recognize those instances when your perspective may interfere with seeing clearly. Consider this experience of a first-grade teacher:

> Travis is one of those kids who is always tapping you on the leg to get your attention. The fact that he is always right there next to me annoys me —maybe it's something about my need for independence. Anyway, I recently found myself in the position of having this kid literally right by my side and realizing I don't know much about him. I'm trying to take a deep breath, accept that he is sticking close because he needs support, and observe to try to get a clearer picture of what is going on with him.

> *What do you bring to observing that helps you tune into the special qualities of each child and build a responsive relationship? What else do you bring that keeps you at a distance and gets in the way of building a relationship?*

Your Culture

Each of us has a set of beliefs about ourselves, as well as attitudes, assumptions, and expectations about people and events around us—some that we may not even be aware of. This is culture; it is what makes each of us who we are. Anthropologist Ward Goodenough (1981) defines culture as "a set of standards or rules for perceiving, believing, acting, and evaluating others."

Our culture is reflected in our communication, expectations, and, therefore, our observations of others. How close you stand when you talk with someone, when you pause for the other person to respond, or if you meet someone's gaze when a person looks at you are examples of behaviors determined by culture. Too often when we think about culture what comes to mind is how holidays are celebrated, what people wear, or what they eat. But culture is much more than holidays, dress, and food and can be subtle.

Indeed, it is so subtle that it influences how we expect people to behave and how we interpret their behavior. When people behave differently from what we expect or when we misinterpret their behavior, we may feel confused, frightened, or even look at them negatively. These feelings get in the way of seeing, getting to know, and relating to a person.

Here are some examples of how cultural differences—or conflicting beliefs—got in the way of teachers as they worked to build relationships with children and families.

Beliefs About Child Rearing

Chloe's toddler son, Georges, sleeps with his parents just as Chloe did when she was a child. Rebecca, Georges's favorite teacher at child care, knows this and cannot accept it. She is constantly hinting that Georges should be sleeping in his own crib. Chloe no longer feels comfortable talking with her. As a result, Rebecca, who spends 8 hours a day, 5 days a week with Georges, is missing out on the opportunity to learn more about Georges's life at home and cannot offer Georges the degree of continuity between home and child care that she could if she and Chloe were working together as partners.

Beliefs About Appropriate Ways to Communicate

At home, dinnertime was filled with busy, interactive conversation during which Isabella's grandmother, mother, father, and sisters all talked continuously, adding to each other's stories as if they were weaving a quilt together. Often several family members talked at once—no one ever thought that adding on to someone's story was an interruption. Isabella came to her preschool classroom eager to share her ideas and experiences and add to the stories of others, just as she does every day at home. However, each time Isabella spoke, her teacher hushed her, saying that she had to raise her hand to talk. At first, Isabella would speak up while simultaneously raising her hand, but this led to more hushing.

After awhile, Isabella stopped talking. In this case of cultural differences, everyone ended up losing. Isabella's enthusiasm about school and her sense of herself as a joyful contributor was diminished. Her teacher's need for order prevented her from connecting with Isabella and teaching her how to be an effective group member at school.

Beliefs About Children's Independence

To Claudia, Rami's behavior was annoying. He worked extremely slowly, demanded her attention, and would not complete tasks independently. Rami and Claudia spent much of his third grade year working against each other—she pushed him to move faster and with more independence and he responded by moving even slower and needing more attention. Although Claudia had a vague sense that Rami's behaviors related to his home life and cultural background, her irritation with him interfered with her willingness to gain support from Rami's mother. On the few occasions when Claudia expressed her frustration about Rami, his mother tried to offer insights. Among other things, she told Claudia that, as the only son, and the youngest child in the family, Rami was not expected to do things on his own. Because of Claudia's frustration and irritation, she wasn't able to hear these explanations, so Rami continued to be a challenge.

Going Beyond Cultural Differences

Like the teachers in these stories, it is easy to assume that your way is the right way. We all do this sometimes. The danger is that it closes you off to seeing other possibilities. When it comes to culture, there are many right ways.

Understanding culture and cultural differences is not easy, even when you have the best intentions and you and the children's families are both invested in the children's well-being and learning.

Here are some strategies that can help you get beyond cultural differences and build trusting relationships:

- Be aware of how your culture—your attitudes, beliefs, and expectations—shapes you as a person and teacher. This will give you some insight into the deep influence culture has on others, including the children and families with whom you work.

- Observe to discover similarities and differences between your culture and those of children and families. Like most of us, you may find similarities easier to deal with than differences. But remember, differences exist and we have to recognize them before we can bridge them. Be open and try to accept and acknowledge both.

- Find out more about what culture means to each family and the ways in which it is reflected in the family's behavior. Continue to observe, listen, and, as trust grows, share some of your questions and your own experiences and beliefs.

Cultural collisions and tensions between teachers and family members are a part of life. If parents of the same child disagree, for example, about the right way to respond to a child's challenging behavior based on how they were raised, it is no surprise that teachers and parents such as Claudia and Rami's mother are caught short by differences, not only between their own cultures, but between the cultures of home and child care or school. The challenge is to get beyond asking what is right and wrong in order to see another person's point of view and communicate openly, always keeping in mind your common goal of supporting the child.

Your Individuality

What and how you see is shaped by who you are. This partially explains how two people can observe the same child and see different things. Through the following stories we explore how different personal characteristics can influence observation.

Temperament

One teacher described how differences in temperament affected how she and the child's parent experienced the child.

> It was early in the year and I was having a conference with Laura's mom. I was ready to share how well I thought Laura was doing in first grade. She had begun to read, she did her work quietly and independently—overall I was really pleased with how she was doing. Her mom began the conference expressing concerns about Laura's shyness. She said that Laura didn't talk much at home—she didn't play with other kids in the neighborhood. Basically, she said that Laura was really different from her older sister and even herself. They were both bubbly—always talking and getting into everything. I thought about this a lot after the conference. I guess you could say I'm a pretty quiet person. I connected with that in Laura. But during the conference—well, it was like we were seeing two different children.

In addition to illustrating how people's perceptions of the same child can be different, the story about Laura describes how much more easily you can connect with a child when the child's way of being in the world matches yours. But what happens when there isn't a match? It can be much harder to observe and appreciate children who are different from you, as you will see from this family child care provider's story.

> Simon is a really active toddler. His idea of a good time is taking two cars and crashing them together. He loves the noise and really gets into it. I can't stand it. As soon as I see him getting the cars from the shelf, I jump in and suggest he try something else.

Someone else observing him might enjoy Simon's enthusiasm and, rather than attempting to change his behavior, might extend his play by showing him how to make a road with long blocks.

Interests

Have you ever gone to a movie with someone and then, when it is over, realize that each of you tuned in to different parts? Perhaps you focused on the characters while your friend was fascinated by the cinematography. Some of us notice the physical aspects of people or things—how people, objects, or places look. Some notice motion and action, others tune into sound or emotions.

Your interests and preferences significantly influence how you see and experience children and how you shape and observe the classroom environment, as illustrated by this teacher's story.

I like lots of activity. When I first started teaching, my classroom was kind of like my home. There were always new projects going on, lots of conversation, and music was often playing. One day, a more experienced teacher commented that things looked a little chaotic as opposed to busy. I had never noticed. But when I stepped back, I could see that he was right. There is still lots going on, but I've learned over the years to observe to see how much activity is the right amount for the children in my group.

Feelings

We encourage you to trust your feelings as an observer. If you feel edgy or a little uncomfortable as you observe a child, it probably means something. Ask more questions, look a little more, and see if you can identify your own feelings, find a way to make a connection, and begin forming a relationship with the child.

Here are two examples of teachers recognizing their own negative feelings about children and using observation to find other ways to look at a child.

There are times I can't see beyond the negative about a child. Sometimes I know what's bugging me. For example, last year there was a girl in my room who loudly demanded my attention. She was hard for me to deal with at first. I could hear my parents telling me, "Ask politely," and at the same time I was a little envious of her boldness. Once I realized this about myself, I could turn my attention to getting to know her. Other times, I'm not so clear on where my feelings about a child are coming from, but I can feel myself getting into a negative pattern. When this happens, I've learned to pull back and go hunting for a positive. I am often surprised to observe a kindness that child has done. I write it down and it changes my mindset about that child.

A boy in my room has occasional seizures. His parents and doctor have given me lots of information and support—but I'm still afraid of him. A few weeks ago, his mother came in all excited because he had taken his first steps over the weekend. I realized for the first time that he is a child first, and a child with seizures second. I began seeing things about him I had never seen before, such as his fascination with our class guinea pigs and how involved he gets in water play. I've decided to take a workshop about working with children with special needs to help me look beyond my fears and see him as he is.

Sometimes it only takes a slight change in perspective to turn negative feelings about a child into more positive ones. Judy tells about a time when she relied on her intuition about Danny, a boy in her third-grade class, rather than focusing on Danny's negative behavior or the reactions he engendered in other staff.

When he entered my class in the fall, Danny already had developed a reputation as a bully, getting into daily fights during recess. Within the first weeks of school his fighting continued as did his trips to the principal's office. I sensed, from observing and talking with him, that he felt bad about this but he didn't have the skills and, more importantly, the confidence he needed to get through an entire recess without a fight. Children Danny's age need to feel competent and when they don't, their feelings of inferiority undermine their success. Danny expected to fail.

As I observed Danny each day, I felt uneasy. On the one hand, I was put off by his surliness—his negative attitude and quick dismissal of my or anyone else's efforts to engage him. Yet at the same time, I felt unsettled—distressed—by what seemed to be his inability to get along with others in the class and, for that matter, to do anything well. Despite the messages I was getting from other adults in the school, I forced myself to listen to the voice inside me that said, this child needs a chance to be special—to do something well. My uneasiness pushed me to take a risk, to reach out to him.

I suggested that he spend recess in the room with me rather than go outside. I told him that it was his choice, not a punishment, but a chance to get through a day without a trip to the office. I offered to show him a special way of painting that I had learned. At first he turned me down, showing his least attractive side. Just before lunch he reconsidered and said he would stay in. We had a really nice time painting together. He enjoyed mixing colors and discovered that he was quite a good painter. Painting became Danny's special talent in our classroom. He taught others how to use the painting technique, spent many recess periods in the room painting, and after awhile we displayed his artwork in the hallway to rave reviews from his peers and other teachers.

In the case of Danny, paying attention to uneasy feelings proved to be just what was needed to form a relationship and give Danny a way to be appreciated. When your feelings about a child are very strong, whether positive or negative, they are a sign to pay attention and observe that child, and your own reactions, more carefully.

Your Professional Expertise

As an educator you bring a great deal to the act of observing—your knowledge, your particular areas of interest and expertise, and your experience. You can rely on these assets and use them to help you learn about children and build relationships with them.

Listen to the comments from two teachers:

> I have a list of developmental guidelines in my head—a kind of mental checklist. When I observe children I tune into how they use their hands and their bodies, how they use language—how long their sentences are. My mental checklist is my lens and, because of my special ed background, my observations are very analytical. I think this makes me a good observer. But one thing I have to watch out for is that I'm not so analytical that I lose sight of the whole. As I observe to learn about each of their skills, I always have to keep in mind that they are not just children who possess a certain set of skills, but unique individuals whom I have to observe over time to really get to know.

> I have spent many years developing my expertise in teaching children to be readers and writers. I tune in immediately to the strategies children use to read and where they are as developing writers. When my first graders are reading and writing, I don't think about trying to actively observe. I'm just doing it all the time—every minute. I feel like I know the right questions to ask them to extend their thinking. I have to work harder to observe children in other areas of the curriculum—subjects where I don't have the same comfort level.

We encourage you to rely on your professional expertise as you observe children. And as these teachers have shared, it is valuable to keep an open mind, knowing that when it comes to observing to learn about children, no one knows it all and we all have more to learn.

Striving for Objectivity

As you have seen, observing has a very human side. No one can be totally objective. However, you can increase your objectivity significantly by differentiating between what you actually see and hear—the facts, and what you think you see—your own opinions and interpretations of these actions.

For example, consider these two different observations of 5-year-old Jason during choice time.

7/13, 11:00 a.m.

Jason chooses to read because he enjoys it.

7/13, 11:00 a.m.

Jason went straight to the reading area during choice time. Began reading Frog and Toad. After a few minutes he looked over to where Doug and Julie were building with blocks. I watched for a few minutes as he watched the children playing. I went over and asked him if he wanted to go play with them. He shook his head and went back to reading his book.

Though both records convey that Jason reads, the first gives only the teacher's impressions. Very often, we observe a child's behavior and think we know what is going on.

However, by describing a child's actions in detail, as illustrated by the second record, the teacher has enough information to ask questions that will lead to supporting Jason: How much time does Jason actually spend reading versus watching the other children? Does he engage in other activities besides reading when given a choice? Does he ever approach children and join in an activity? Is there something I can do to help him feel more comfortable in other areas of the room? Consider these examples:

Jerome, a kindergarten teacher, has recorded this observation about Omar, who is drawing and writing about the class trip to the apple orchard.

2/13, Omar: Drawing and Writing

Selects 3 crayons from box. Rolls them on table. Looks around. Picks up crayon from floor. Makes a few marks on paper. Walks to the window—back to table. Looks at Richard's paper. To Richard, "Whatchya drawing? I'm gonna make apples." Uses green crayon to draw a circle, pressing hard, scribbles in color.

Miriam, a kindergarten teacher, has recorded this observation about Justine working on a collage:

4/21:, Justine: Art Table

J is confused and frustrated. She is not relaxed or enjoying the assignment. After a few minutes she gets up and leaves the table, leaving the task incomplete.

> *What do you notice about the two*
> *observational records?*

Jerome was objective. He noted what actually happened—what he saw and heard Omar do. Miriam focused on her interpretations of Justine's actions—what she thought Justine was thinking and feeling.

Can Miriam actually know if Justine was confused, frustrated, tense, or not enjoying the activity just from watching her?

Instead of Miriam's interpretations becoming conclusions, they can be questions that require further exploration. For example, after observing, Miriam might wonder: Is Justine confused or frustrated? Did she not enjoy the task? If not, why not? These questions might prompt Miriam to engage Justine in conversation. Or, she might observe Justine using different materials to see if her behavior is the same or different.

When you record your observations, you can make room for your questions and interpretations. As we discussed earlier in this chapter, your impressions and feelings can add rich insights. Just be sure to identify them as such. Some teachers divide their records into two parts, as illustrated in the example below. They write observations on one side, and on the other they note questions, concerns, and interpretations.

Notes	Interpretations
7/13: 11:00 a.m.—Jason went straight to the reading area during choice time. Began reading Frog and Toad. After a few minutes he looked over to where Doug and Julie were building with blocks. I watched for a few minutes as he watched the children playing. I went over and asked him if he wanted to go play with them. He shook his head and went back to reading his book	Reading or avoiding approaching other children? Why not?

The strategies we offer below can help you be as objective and effective an observer as possible.

Tune In to Individual Children

The story of who children are—what makes them unique individuals—comes to light through the details you collect about them over time. As two teachers describe it:

> Observation by observation, bit by bit, a picture of a child unfolds and continues to blossom throughout the year.

◆　◆　◆　◆　◆　◆

Before I began using an observational assessment, I tended to get the big picture of things in my classroom. I always said that I knew my kids really well. I could tell you who talked a lot at circle time, who was quiet, who did the work, who always forgot assignments. But once I started to observe more, I realized how much I didn't know about them. I started paying attention more—noticing little details about what they said, how they interacted with each other, how they went about tasks. I can tell you really specific details about each child now.

Tuning in to each child and observing for details can be a challenge for at least two reasons. First, if your classroom is like our classrooms were, you're always on the go, answering at least two children's questions at once, helping another to find a missing puzzle piece, and constantly monitoring to be sure that everyone is safe and engaged. Having so many demands on your time can make it difficult to focus and, as a result, can lead to superficial observations. In addition, because you spend the majority of your waking hours in your classroom with the same children, it can be hard to pay close attention to what you see all the time.

Observing details requires slowing down and looking with care. Consider the contrast between Ms. Jennings' intentions and the results of her actions in the examples below.

When Brian calls Ms. Jennings over to show her his painting, she rushes over, glances at it quickly, and says, "Nice job, Brian," as she hurries off to Laurie, who has asked for help with the computer. In her haste, she misses an important opportunity to observe and use what she sees to connect with Brian and have a meaningful conversation about his work.

Now imagine that Ms. Jennings slows down for a moment, takes a careful look at Brian's painting, and says, "Brian, tell me about your painting. What do you like about it?" She waits while he considers his response. Through this interaction Ms. Jennings shows her sincere interest in Brian's work and asks for his opinions. Brian has a chance to feel good about himself and reflect on his creation because Ms. Jennings took a moment to tune in to Brian and his work.

Describe Rather Than Label Children's Behavior

All of us rely on labeling words such as shy, aggressive, helpful, cooperative, annoying to describe people and actions because labels are quick and easy to use. They are right there, on the tip of our tongues. Consider this teacher's description of a child: "Tiara is withdrawn."

> *Based on this teacher's words, what do you imagine Tiara is like?*

Each of us has social constructions or meanings for words that are based on our experiences and our culture. However, the behaviors that cause us to label a child can reflect many different meanings. Consider the following behaviors and reasons why a teacher might describe a child as withdrawn:

- She was quiet because she needs some help getting adjusted to a new situation.

- She was playing alone because she needs to learn strategies for engaging with other children.

- She was tired because she didn't sleep well the night before.

- She was sad because her cat died recently.

As you can see, labeling a child as withdrawn could be misleading. Moreover, your feelings and attitudes about what "withdrawn" means determine your response.

Earlier in this chapter we discussed how assumptions trigger scripts that affect children's behavior and the attitudes of other children—and even adults—around them. Let's think about how this might work with Tiara:

> *What might you say or do when you see her sitting away from a group of children, head down, playing with some colored cubes? How might she respond? What will the other children learn about Tiara based on your actions or comments? How might they then behave toward her? What if you had a conference with Tiara's parents and described her as "withdrawn" rather than describing the behaviors that led you to that conclusion? How might they feel about Tiara? About you?*

As you can see, labels can have a powerful ripple effect on a child's self-esteem and the attitudes of others toward that child. Labels do not reveal the specific characteristics that make each child unique.

Instead of using the word "withdrawn" to describe Tiara, imagine what you can learn about her by taking a little more time and using a few more words to elaborate on the behaviors you see that lead you to say she is withdrawn. For example, observations of Tiara watching but not speaking may lead you to discover that she does not know how to enter a group. Asking her parents how much she interacts at home may give you a picture of a very animated child interacting easily with her siblings.

What you can learn about a child is endless. The point is, when you use labels you limit the possibilities, which also limits your ability to get to know a child better and to support that child's success as a learner.

Listen to Children

We often think we know how children feel or what they are thinking just from watching them. But because we can't be inside a child's mind, we can never know for sure. So what do we do? One solution is to go directly to the source. Children can be an amazing source of information about what they are thinking or feeling—if we just take the time to listen and ask questions.

As you'll see in the following examples, listening can take varied forms, depending on the age of a child and the situation. In the two examples below, teachers tell about listening to children who didn't say a word. They are learning about children by listening to them and reading the meaning of their expressions, gestures, and how they move:

> Vanessa, who just turned 4 months old last week, is a new child in our program. Yesterday she was fussy and I figured she was tired. I laid her in her crib and gently patted her back like I do with other babies. Inch by inch, she began squinching up away from my hand toward the corner of the crib. I think she may be one of those kids who is sensitive to touch. I'm going to talk with her parents and observe to see if I'm right.

Arrival is a really important observation time for me. I observe kids as they come into the room in the morning. I look to see if they have a certain look—are they scowling, do they seem tired? I decide just how to respond. Sometimes I will take the child aside and say, "So, what's going on?" Usually this helps a lot. But other times, I don't ask questions. Like with Jasmine. The other day she came in looking really upset. I decided that she needed a little extra attention and maybe some TLC. I didn't know what was wrong but, knowing her, asking wouldn't be the way to go. So, I greeted her warmly and suggested that when she was ready, perhaps she could feed the fish. As the morning wore on, she relaxed and settled into the day.

Group discussions and one-on-one conversations are only two of the many opportunities to learn who children are and what they know by listening to them. These examples illustrate how teachers learn by listening to children:

Tiffany is 4. She was busily at work in dramatic play. She and two other children were using props to play "firehouse." Tiffany declared with authority, "Uh oh, that's the alarm. Hey you guys, put on your coats and boots. We better get the truck ready and get out of here in a hurry." Tiff rarely speaks up in group discussions, so I had no idea how much she had learned during our trip to the fire station. It was just one of those lucky moments that I happened to be listening while they were in dramatic play.

As children work I wander around and sort of eavesdrop on their conversations. I am always amazed by how much they learn from each other. The other day, while working on their math, Shawna was giving Marie advice about how to settle a fight with Jocelyn. I was really impressed with Shawna's suggestions and with how thoughtfully Marie was listening. I wouldn't have pegged Shawna as one to give such good advice.

Learn From Families

Families can help you get a clearer picture of their child by sharing information and responding to insights and questions based on what you observe.

You and families each bring different sets of information to your relationship. You have worked with many children of similar ages over the years. You know about general patterns of child development and have developed a collection of strategies to support children's learning. Parents or other family members focus on "their" child. They know the specific information about that one special child in their life. For example, they know about their child's culture, preferences, fears, and how their child responds in certain situations at home. To know a child, you need both sets of information. But you will never know what a family knows unless you exchange information, ask questions, and listen to one another. Like the teacher below, you may be surprised at what you learn:

> When Nicky came in on Tuesday, we noticed his gait had a peculiar swing to it. We watched and began worrying that maybe he had developed some sort of neurological problem. That afternoon, Nicky's father came to pick him up. I asked him how things were going at home and he started talking about repairing the deck on his father's boat. Nicky had spent the long weekend with his grandparents who live on a houseboat, and his gait reflected the gentle rock of the boat!

When you share observations with parents you can sharpen your picture of a child by validating, expanding, or calling into question something you have seen.

> *Remember Rami and Claudia (page 35)? How do you think Rami's school experience would have been different if Claudia had been able to hear what his mother was saying and as a result put aside her assumptions and seen Rami's behavior in a new way?*

Communicating effectively with parents doesn't mean you have to be best friends, or even like one another—though that certainly makes life easier. What it does mean is that you have to see yourselves as partners with the child's best interests as your shared concern.

This isn't always easy. Sharing the care and education of children can stir up deep emotions, including jealousy, competition, and resentment. Have you ever had fleeting thoughts such as: "If this were my child, her clothes would be clean" or "If this parent were better at setting limits, his child wouldn't be disrupting the group"? We all have. These feelings usually stem from our attachment and commitment to children—qualities children need from their teachers. Yet they can interfere with the open communication between families and teachers that children also need. We're not suggesting you eliminate these feelings—you can't. We're simply encouraging you to be aware of them so they don't get in the way of the child's best interests.

Like all relationships, those with families take time to develop and require work to maintain. But they are well worth it.

Finally, Keep Track of How You Are Doing

Observing objectively requires ongoing vigilance. Using the strategies mentioned above will help, but they are no guarantee you will always see children for the unique individuals they are.

Because observing is such a personal endeavor, it is no wonder that sometimes it is more difficult to separate your experiences, feelings, and assumptions from what you are seeing. Being tired, upset about something, or under stress can make it a challenge to step back and be impartial.

To help you be as objective an observer as possible, we recommend regularly checking in to give yourself an "objectivity tune-up." Ask yourself:

- Have I gathered sufficient observational data to form a conclusion?

- Am I aware of how my feelings might be influencing what I'm seeing?

- Am I taking enough time before I label or interpret?

If you have doubts, enlist the assistance of a colleague. Ask that person to observe with you, then to confirm or call into question what you have seen. Even if you don't have doubts, observing with a colleague every now and then can help you be sure you are seeing what is, not just what you think is there. The children you teach deserve no less.

Teacher judgment and decision making form the core of good classroom practice. As we discuss later in the book, you make on-the-spot judgments and decisions throughout the day. But, when making judgments about children—who they are, what they know, and how they learn best—it is important to make informed judgments that are based on sufficient evidence. Descriptive information and information collected by talking with children and their families provides you with the evidence you need to feel confident that your judgments are accurate.

SUMMING UP

We can never eliminate the personal side of observing, nor would that be a good idea. At the same time, you need to be aware of it because what you bring to observing shapes how you see children and families, which in turn, affects your relationships with them and the decisions you make. To help you be sure that your pictures of children and your relationships with them reflect reality rather than your assumptions about them:

- **Be aware of what you bring to observing**—your culture, temperament, interests, feelings, and professional expertise. This will increase the chances that your observations will give you insight into who children are and that your relationships with them will be authentic.

- **Strive for objectivity.** Strategies to help you be an objective and effective observer include tuning into individual children, describing rather than labeling children's behavior, listening to children, learning from families, and keeping track of how you are doing by giving yourself an "objectivity tune-up."

In the next chapter, we look at guidelines for effective observation.

Guidelines for Effective Observation

What do you think about when you hear the word observing? When we ask teachers how they picture "classroom observation," they usually describe a teacher or caregiver sitting or standing with clipboard in hand, showing little or no facial expression, ignoring comments and social overtures from the children. Many of us see ourselves outside the action, clipboard in hand, taking notes. As you will see, this is only one way to observe. There are many other ways to learn about children:

- Watch them with family members when they arrive and at the end of the day.

- Observe them as they engage in daily routines, jotting down what they do or say.

- Watch them as they play and work with materials and other children, making some notes about what you see.

- Talk with them about what they are doing or making—for example, when they explore playdough, paint, write, or build with blocks.

- Ask questions that encourage them to describe their thinking and listen carefully to their responses.

- Listen as they talk with others informally and during group discussions, jotting down notes about what they say.

- Study their work (e.g., projects, constructions, drawings, writing, journals).

- Observe them during home visits.

- Talk with family members to learn their children's likes and dislikes or special interests.

These ways of learning about children point to four guidelines for effective observation: observe over time; watch children in varied situations; keep track of what you observe; and observe in and out of the action.

Observe Over Time

One observation can never give you a complete picture. Only after observing over time are you able to see a child's growth and progress. Consider this analogy:

Imagine for a moment that you are planting daffodil bulbs. Someone passes by and asks you what you're doing. Amazingly enough, the passerby has never seen a daffodil before. You show her the bulb and she observes it carefully. She sees something round and brown with a little shoot sticking out. You encourage her to pass by a few more times to study the daffodil: first in the early spring to see the long green leaves and the tightly closed bloom; then perhaps a week or two later to see the bright yellow blossom; and maybe one month later to see drooping leaves. Despite the passerby's one-time careful observation of the bulb, you know that she must observe the daffodil over time to see it grow and change.

The same holds true for children. Observing the same child more than once, over time, will enable you to see that child change and grow. More limited observation will only tell part of the story.

Each time you observe a child, you learn something important. For example, you might watch a mobile infant using a chair to pull himself up. This event prompts you to double check nearby furniture for sharp corners and steadiness. Or you might see that a first grader uses her fingers to count to 10. As a result of this observation, the first-grade teacher can build on the child's strategy of using fingers to show her how to count to 20. Each observational moment gives you information that you can use to help the child grow and learn.

A student teacher shared this story with us about Pam, age 7:

> My first week of student teaching, there was a little girl who stood apart from the group, over behind the bookshelf during circle time. In my notes, I wrote: "Pam—Doesn't participate." Privately I thought she was really out of it. I was worried about her.
>
> I asked my cooperating teacher, Alisa, why she didn't ask Pam to join the group. We talked about Pam's generally cautious temperament and her reluctance to join structured group activities. Alisa explained to me that sometimes the best way to support an individual child and the group is to ignore a behavior and proceed with the lesson.
>
> We observed Pam for the next few weeks. To my surprise, I saw a child who was very engaged. Pam nodded yes when Alisa asked if everyone had read Chapter Two. She raised her hand and answered a question—all from her spot at the bookshelf. We observed that Pam interacted quite comfortably with individual children. It seemed to be the large-group, structured activities that threw her.
>
> Then one day, about a month into the year, Pam came out from behind the bookshelf and sat on the floor in front of the shelf during a group discussion. A week later, Alisa patted the floor inviting Pam to sit next to her. Pam looked away, then back at Alisa and slowly walked over and sat down. She was quiet that day and the next. But by the end of the semester, when it was time for me to leave, Pam shared regularly in group time. This little girl I had been so concerned about was just fine.

If the student teacher had not observed over time, she would have never been alert to the subtle ways Pam was participating.

Watch Children in Varied Situations

Think of how you act in different situations. In settings where you are comfortable, you may be outgoing and talkative. In other less familiar ones, you may hold back and be reluctant to share your thoughts. Children also behave differently in varied situations. For example, 11-month-old Melissa falls asleep easily on the cushions in the reading corner, but puts up a struggle when her caregiver tries to lay her down in her crib for a nap. Craig, age 5, comes to life outdoors, taking initiative in inventing games and organizing his friends. Eight-year-old Khalan speaks easily to friends and family at home, but remains quiet and reserved in the classroom.

Observing in different situations gives us a more complete understanding of who a child is and what that child knows and can do. As one teacher said:

> I love putting all the information together and creating a picture of the child. After I started consciously trying to observe in different situations and over time, I realized I had been blind and not seeing the whole.

What factors should you consider as you attempt to observe children in varied situations? Here are a few suggestions.

Social Settings

The size of a group and the child's familiarity with group members are likely to influence behavior. Consider these examples. Jenny, age 3, speaks easily with her teacher when they read a story alone together, but is shy and reserved when asked a question in front of her peers. On a class field trip, 8-year-old Paul readily asks the naturalist (someone he has never met before) questions about the fish, whereas Justin, usually bursting with questions for his teacher or classmates, is very quiet.

Time of Day

You have probably noticed that children behave differently at different times during the day. For example, think about the infant who is alert in the morning and more drowsy in the afternoon. Or, a tired and grumpy 4-year-old who won't join the group for a story first thing in the morning, but is an eager group participant after snack.

Individual Preferences

Children's preferences, like ours, affect their comfort level and attitude and, thus, their behavior. Some children like to build, others prefer painting, still others are most comfortable talking and writing. Some light up at a cooking activity and others when read to aloud. To observe what children know and can do, we have to get to know their preferences and then watch them in these situations. Consider this example from Maria, a kindergarten teacher:

> I was convinced that Shaquin had a language problem because she rarely spoke during group time, one-on-one, or even in small groups. When she did, it was one or two words, no complete sentences, and very limited vocabulary. One day I was observing the children in dramatic play where they had set up a beauty parlor. I heard Shaquin chatting away enthusiastically, questioning one of her customers: "How short should I cut your hair? Do you want me to dye it lighter than last time?" On reflection I realized that Shaquin often chose dramatic play during work time and was more verbal doing something she enjoys.

Degree of Choice

Sometimes children's behavior is affected by whether they have chosen an activity. When children select activities they are interested in and care about, they are likely to engage more readily and with greater enthusiasm than teacher-directed activities as this story from a kindergarten teacher shows:

I was preparing for a family conference and I couldn't think of anything positive to say about Derrek. I knew my concerns clearly and planned to share with his mother that he was contrary, obstinate, and unwilling to follow my directions—obviously not using those words! I forced myself to study my observation notes and samples of his work. Most of my notes described his behavior problems. However, I did notice a few examples of carefully completed work, particularly drawings he had made during choice time and put into his portfolio. One drawing was a very detailed picture of a ship—he used pencil and crayons. I didn't think he had such well-developed fine motor skills because when I ask him to write, mostly he scribbles. I realized then that I had to work on giving Derrek more choices and control over his work, even when I'm directing the activity. I also decided to share the drawing with his mom at the beginning of the conference.

Level of Competence

Children who feel competent are more likely to experiment and engage in new activities. For example, 23-month-old Elliot, who has parents and caregivers who give him many opportunities to experience success, climbs to the top of the new slide in the park and calls out, "Me do it!" First grader Yi-Ping, who also has developed a sense of confidence, volunteers to read aloud from a new book.

> *Try observing one or two children for a few days, noting how their behaviors vary depending on the situation. Are their actions the same regardless of the situation? Or do they vary depending on whom they are interacting with, where they are, and the time of day? Are their actions affected by their preferences, whether they have chosen an activity, and how confident or competent they feel to complete the activity?*

Keep Track of What You Observe

Writing something down makes you pay attention to it. Recording your observations will help you tune into nuance and detail that you might otherwise miss. When you write things down, you can keep track of a child's development over time. You can identify and reflect on patterns that will give you a clearer picture of the whole child. Here's what some caregivers, teachers, and family child care providers say about recording:

> My anecdotal notes are little glimpses into children's personalities, which, if I didn't write down, I wouldn't recall.

> Writing stuff down allows me to focus better on the child. I remember more details. I look at my notes and recall how long the situation lasted, how long the child stayed with a task. I write really brief notes—sometimes just a word or two.

If the thought of writing is intimidating for you, relax. Chapter 5 describes many different techniques you can use to document observations. We also want to point out that observing is valuable, whether or not you record what you see. As one caregiver said:

> I observe all the time without taking notes—it's all observing and all meaningful.

Remember, the goal is to be a careful observer so that you get to know children well. Writing something down makes you more intentional. But don't feel as if you have to write a great deal; a few words, a phrase or two will help you keep track of what you observe. Give yourself assignments so that your recording has a purpose. For example, observe and record examples of ways children use language to describe. Or, decide to pay attention to children's scientific thinking. Try to record the type of questions children ask or the predictions they make. The key is to focus on something you find interesting or that you need to know.

Observe In and Out of the Action

Most often, we think of observing as happening when we are not a part of classroom activities. The benefit of stepping out of the action is that you can temporarily put down all the balls you are juggling and focus on who or what you are observing. It doesn't have to take a great deal of time. You will be surprised by how much data you can collect by taking 3 to 5 minutes to observe one or two children a few times each week.

However, stepping out of the action is often not feasible in the midst of a busy child care setting or classroom. Having other options in mind can help you observe more regularly. Here are two other approaches.

Observe While Participating in the Action

You are typically in the midst of the action. You might be changing a diaper, making a batch of playdough with a small group of 2-year-olds, conferring with a student about his writing, guiding a small group through a math lesson, or having a discussion with your class about transportation in your city.

At the same time, you are watching children, listening to them, taking mental notes about who is doing what, and asking questions that extend children's learning and thinking. Clearly, you are gathering a wealth of information. The first challenge you face when you are at your busiest is how to focus enough on what you're observing so that you will remember some of it. Even at these very busy times, we encourage you to give yourself permission to slow down a bit, take a deep breath, and notice more consciously what one child is doing, even if you miss another child's activities.

A second challenge is figuring out how you can record some of what you see so that you don't have to rely solely on your memory. In this situation you can probably only record a few words, or make check marks or other symbols on a class list. But even if you don't get to write something down, just being more conscious will help you get to know your children better. The next chapter offers many different ideas about how to capture a quick note when you are participating in the action.

Reflect on the Action After the Fact and Make Some Notes

Reflecting after the fact is often the most practical way to record what you see and hear in a busy center or classroom. You probably make mental notes in the midst of the action all the time. By taking a few minutes during a break in the day (e.g., during rest time, quiet reading, or journal time) or at the end of the day, you can record brief notes about events that occurred. Recall how various children responded to the sights and sounds of a neighborhood walk, the strategies children used to solve math problems, or children's comments during a discussion about recycling. A preschool teacher shares how she reflects after the fact:

> I take a lot of photographs during the course of the week. I revisit them with the children and alone. I write things down as I look at the photos when I have time during the day or at the end of the day.

If you work with preschool and school-age children, you probably spend time reviewing their work at the end of the day or week. Make some notes about what you see. Looking at the work will remind you of events related to its creation. You are likely to recall:

- How the child went about the task
- The child's interest level
- Whether the child worked alone or with others
- What else was happening in the classroom at the time

To be a successful observer, we must broaden our image of observing beyond watching from the sidelines to include observing and recording while participating with children and reflecting and jotting down notes after the fact.

SUMMING UP

We learn about children by carefully watching them, listening to them, and studying their work. Watching and listening to them helps us understand what they are feeling, learning, and thinking. Here are four guidelines to help you be an effective observer:

- **Observe over time.** Observing the same child over time enables you to see that child change and grow.

- **Watch children in varied situations.** Like you, children may act differently according to the situation. Such factors as the social setting, time of day, individual preferences, degree of choice, and level of competence may influence a child's behavior.

- **Keep track of what you see.** This will help you become a more intentional observer, notice patterns, and obtain a more complete picture of the child.

- **Observe in and out of the action.** Don't limit yourself by thinking that you can only observe when you step out of the action. Observe while participating in the action, reflect on the action after the fact, and/or make some notes.

The next chapter discusses the many decisions you make every day about observing, including selecting your "tools of the trade."

Becoming a Skilled Observer

Effective observing doesn't just happen. It involves thoughtful planning—an ongoing process of asking questions and making decisions. "How can you expect me to stop and think about when and how to observe in the middle of a busy day when I have hundreds of other things to think about?" you may ask. We don't. We have learned that effective observing requires planning: making decisions in advance about what and how you want to observe.

As you become a more experienced observer, your questioning, decision making, and planning become second nature—a part of your ongoing thinking process. There will be times when you have to pause and struggle a bit to be sure you get the information and insight you need. But the wonderful thing about observing is that it is (at least it should be) an ongoing practice, so if you miss something today you can catch it tomorrow.

This chapter identifies and discusses questions to consider and decisions to make with regard to effective observing. Being aware of these questions and thinking about them ahead of time will increase your chances of finding out what you want to know about children, families, and yourself as a teacher. Don't be surprised to discover you are asking yourself these questions every day—perhaps without realizing it.

- What do I want to find out?

- When and where should I observe to get the information I need?

- How do I record what I observe?

- How do I organize the information I collect?

What Do I Want to Find Out?

As a teacher, you are aware of and open to what is going on around you. You are engaged in an ongoing process of asking questions, gathering information, and reflecting on and hypothesizing about what you observe. You will recall that in chapter 2 we discussed questions that help you get to know children in order to build relationships with them. We described observation as the process of asking questions and answering questions. The questions you ask change continually, depending on a variety of factors including how well you know a child, the child's stage of development, and the specific issues of a child or family.

Sometimes you will know who or what you want to learn more about and ask yourself very clear questions to guide your observing. The chart on the opposite page has some examples of these questions.

Other times, your questions may be harder to put into words—or you may not even be aware that you have a question. Caregivers and teachers we've spoken with describe observing in these instances as "open observing," as trying "to get a feel for a child," "to better understand what a child is experiencing," and "to get a sense of what is going on." Listen as two teachers describe this type of observing:

> You are open to what a child may bring, getting inside his head, by noticing all of the child's cues.

To learn more about:	You may ask questions such as:
An individual child	• What is this child's temperament? • How does this child interact with others? • What does Johnny know about monarch butterflies?
A family	• How does Rachita's family promote her language development? • How does a family feel about promoting independence (e.g., does Kyle's mother encourage him to put on and fasten his own coat or does she do it for him to be nurturing)? • How involved is Baili's family in helping her do her homework?
Particular skills or content	• How can the toddlers participate in lunchtime? • What do children know about patterns? • In what ways are children using revision strategies in their writing?
Group dynamics	• How is the transition between lunch and nap time going? • Who is working/playing with whom during morning center time? • What's going on with the group during recess that is causing so many kids to come back to the room angry?
The physical environment	• How can I arrange the shelves so children can make clear choices about what they want to play with? • How can I change the block area to avoid so many toppled buildings and arguments during work times? • How can I modify the environment to promote more collaborative group work?

To learn more about:	You may ask questions such as:
The effectiveness of your planning, interactions, and instruction	• How do the children respond to the way I set limits? • How do the children respond to the stories I'm reading to them? • Did children understand the directions I gave for completing their science projects?

◆   ◆   ◆   ◆   ◆   ◆

> You come in with a blank picture. You observe and the pieces come together. You need to be open to what you see. As you watch and interact, a relationship forms. Then you can observe for particulars. With free-form observing, you gain greater appreciation of how kids see the world—of their individual styles and your impact on kids. It helps you see through their eyes—to see them grow.

We know from our own experience that this "open" observing is a way of being with children. As described in chapter 2, as teachers observe, they engage with children and build relationships with them. Teachers speak passionately about the experience. "You're connected by an invisible thread," one told us. In the words of another, "It is as if you feel a child. You become a part of them, they become a part of you."

We encourage you to consider the idea that when you observe in this way, you are asking a question, even if you haven't put it into words. Your question may be as open as "Who is this child?" or "How are things going?" or "That looks interesting, what's happening here?"—but it is still a question.

Putting what you want to learn into a question provides you with a clear purpose as an observer. It is also the heart of assessment. As one family child care provider told us:

It really helps me see that, when I'm observing, I'm
doing important work.

Being aware of your question doesn't have to detract from the
wonder of what you see or feel as you get to know a child.
Indeed, it often makes the experience richer and more gratifying.
You will know that your observation is not something that just
happened. Instead, your skills as an observer and listener combine
with your knowledge of child development and allow you to
watch as individual children discover something new about the
world around them.

You should realize that stating a question doesn't guarantee that
you will find the answer immediately. Indeed, there are bound to
be times when you can't see—at least in the short term—what you
have learned. Other times you might feel slightly overwhelmed
by images and information that don't immediately make sense.
When this happens, keep watching. Continue reflecting and
hypothesizing about what you have noticed. Observe again.
Eventually the information you collect will become part of a
bigger picture and lead to new questions and new observations.

Think about your most recent observations. What are
some of the questions you have been trying to answer?

When and Where Should I Observe?

There will be times when you can plan when and where to observe.
For example, if you want to see how 18-month-old Louis is handling
separation, observe him at the beginning and end of the day when
his grandmother drops him off and picks him up. To discover what
Amanda, age 4, knows about patterns, you can introduce pattern
blocks to her during choice time. And to help you assess the sense of
community among your second graders, you can observe interaction
during group discussion and work time.

Sometimes you figure out the when and where on the spur of the moment—for example, when you observe because you see or hear something that strikes you as curious or simply because you have a free minute. Because children express what they are feeling and learning throughout the day, being open—to the expected and unexpected—means that you catch many small moments that add up to a greater understanding of the children you care so much about. As you help a child get ready for a nap, you may glance up to see Louis shoring up his sense of connection with home as he wanders over to the family pictures hanging on the wall and touches the one of his mother. Amanda's ability to duplicate patterns may be demonstrated when she arranges raisins and pretzel sticks on her placemat at snack time. Or a developing sense of community may be revealed when you overhear three children talking after recess about how to include other children in tomorrow's kickball game. Observing spontaneously can reveal a great deal of information about children.

Include planning for observation as part of your daily and weekly schedule. We're not suggesting a great deal of extra writing. For example, if you want to know more about how Louis handles separation throughout the day, jot down "Louis—separation?" on Monday and Wednesday. During those days, keep an eye on him to see if he is playing peek-a-boo, calling home on the toy phone, talking about his parents, or engaging in any other behaviors that help toddlers feel some control over hellos and good-byes and connected with those they love. If you are wondering what Amanda knows about measurement, jot down "Amanda—measuring" next to the cooking activity you have planned for Thursday. These small reminders will help you find out what you want to know.

This illustration shows a segment of a first-grade teacher's plan book. She includes plans for observation by making notes to remind her of what or whom she wants to observe. On Monday, she plans to introduce the week's unit on measurement during the morning meeting. She records children's responses on a chart, keeping track of who said what. Her note "make grid" is a reminder that she needs to make a matrix (see pages 80–81) to observe and document specific skills. After reviewing some of her observational notes from the previous week, she decides to check in with children she hasn't conferenced with for 2 weeks. When the children go to the library, her observations are focused by her question, "Who has a plan?"

4/5 Monday

8:15 Morning meeting -
- intro measuring
"Why do you think we have rulers and other measuring tools?" (record comments on chart)

8:30 Math work time - (make grid)
- using string & non-standard unit of choice, measure body lengths.

9:10 Writers workshop - check in w/ Ryan, Brett, Lori, SheKoya

10:00 Library - who has a plan?
- Jessica, Trey, Bobby ???

How Do I Record What I Observe?

There are many ways to record observational data. Each technique makes different demands on your time and energy, and each provides a different kind of information. The decision about what methods to use depends on what you want to learn, the activities children are engaged in, and your responsibilities at the time you are observing. And, of course, how you record must match your personal style. This section provides you with a variety of options and highlights ways teachers have used them successfully.

As you can see from the comments of these two teachers, some use many methods and others rely on only one or two:

> I use all different methods and tools, depending on what and when I'm observing. Mostly I grab stickies and just jot down a quick note so I can remember it later.

> I keep a small spiral notebook with me all the time and jot down what I see.

One first-grade teacher told us:

> When I have a conversation with a child that I want to remember, I need to make a note—I'll write down a few words so I don't forget what we talked about—otherwise it's gone. When I'm planning lessons I make grids. I write the names of the kids I want to observe and list four or five things I want to observe for. Doing this helps my observations stay focused.

Overall, most caregivers and teachers say they use a few different methods, rather than just one. For example, when observing a child's mood, thinking process, method for solving a problem, way of using materials, and quality of interactions with others, select a method that allows for some descriptive writing. On the other hand, if you simply want to record the materials a child selects to help solve a math problem, or the colors a child names accurately, it is more efficient to use a method that allows you to make checks or tally marks.

When you are working one-on-one with a child, reading a book together, or having a writing conference, you have the time to take rich notes that describe the child's actions and words. However, when circulating to guide children's learning during a science activity, making quick check marks on a matrix is easier to manage.

We describe several different methods below and show some examples of each.

Brief Notes

Brief notes, the most common way teachers record their observations, are quick written records that serve as a reminder of observed events. Teachers typically record these notes on sticky notes, index cards, mailing labels, or whatever piece of paper happens to be close at hand.

Brief Notes on Mailing Labels

A preschool teacher jotted these brief notes about the children she teaches on a sheet of mailing labels she keeps handy on a clipboard. At the end of the week she'll peel the labels off and place each label in that child's section of a binder she uses to store her observations.

Brief Notes on Index Cards

A first-grade teacher wrote a set of brief notes during one week to keep track of Alex's reading and writing. She records notes about all of her students on index cards attached to a file folder. When she fills up a card, she transfers it to her file on that child and replaces it with a new card.

Brief Notes on a Daily Log

An infant–toddler caregiver created this form to use to exchange news and observations with families about their child's day.

DAILY LOG

Child's name: **Jason**   Date: **11/3**

NEWS FROM HOME -
How did your child sleep last night?
Well **X** Woke up in the night _____ How much? **A few**
When did your child last eat? **7:00**
spoonfuls of cereal
Who will pick up your child today? **Grandma** When? **5:00**
Medication today? Yes _____ No **X**
Special instructions: _____
Anything happening in your child's life we need to know?
Jason's grandparents are visiting for
the week.

NEWS FROM CHILDCARE -
Medication? Yes _____ No **X**   When? _____
Your child ate: **french toast**   When? **10:00 a.m.**
Sandwich and pear   When? **11:30 a.m.**
peanut butter & crackers   When? **3:00 p.m.**
_____   When? _____

Your child slept from: **12:30** to **2:30**
_____ to _____

Your child had a b.m. Yes _____ No **X**
Today your child enjoyed: **Collecting stones in his pail,**
watching a squirrel, doing a puzzle and going
through the obstacle course we made.
Please remember to bring in : diapers _____ wipes _____
set of clean clothes _____ Other: **family photos for our album**

Thanks. See you tomorrow!

From *Prime Times: A Handbook for Excellence in Infant and Toddler Programs* by J. Greenman and A. Stonehouse, 1996, St. Paul: MN: Redleaf Press, p. 284. Adapted with permission.

Anecdotal Notes

Anecdotal notes are more detailed, narrative accounts that
describe a particular event factually. Often they are created by
jotting down brief notes and adding details later. The following
illustration is an anecdotal record from an infant caregiver who
observed Victor's (12 months) reunion with his father at the end
of the day.

> **Victor**   4/29
>
> V. is spinning a knob on the busy box and vocalizing. He
> pulls himself up to stand on the snack table, then gets
> down on all fours and crawls to the toy shelf. Still
> vocalizing, he heads back towards the busy box and comes
> face to face with his dad's legs. He quiets, sits, looks
> up at Dad, smiles, then turns away. Dad bends
> down and touches his cheek. V. raises his arms to
> be picked up. Dad lifts him off the floor and V.
> goes into his arms willingly, clutching Dad's
> jacket in one fist.

Here is an example of an anecdotal note describing several children.

Obs. for 4 min.
During Center Time

Children observed: Shelby, Maddy, Andrea, Shanese, Desiree + Teresse

Daily Observation
11/2

Maddy and Shelby decided to put on a puppet show. Maddy directed Andrea, Shanese, Desiree, and Teresse where to sit. They sat where she directed them. Teresse got up and moved to the rocking chair, saying over and over, "I can't see." Maddy opened the curtains of the puppet stage and she and Shelby performed the story of the Little Red Riding Hood. As Shelby moved the puppets, she knocked down some props on the stage. Maddy declared, "Shelby! Now look." Shelby quickly picked them up. Shelby was Little Red Riding Hood; Maddy was mom. When they finished acting out the story, Desiree said, "I want to see it again." Teresse said, "I want to see it tomorrow." Maddy said, "I'm not going to do it again until you're all sitting down the right way. She waited until all the girls were seated. They began the puppet play again. Teresse stayed and listened.

Running Records

Running records are detailed narrative accounts of behavior recorded in a sequential manner, exactly as it happens. They include all behavior that occurs within a given time frame. Like anecdotal notes, they provide rich information, but require you to step out of the action.

In this example, a second-grade teacher observes David working at the classroom bookstore, then reflects on what she has learned and how she will use this information. She wanted this degree of detail to help her prepare for a conference with David's family.

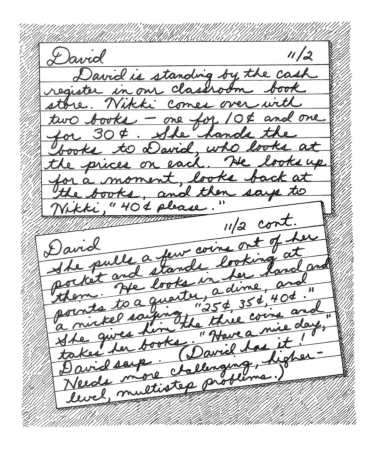

David   11/2

David is standing by the cash register in our classroom book store. Nikki comes over with two books — one for 10¢ and one for 30¢. She hands the books to David, who looks at the prices on each. He looks up for a moment, looks back at the books, and then says to Nikki, "40¢ please."

11/2 cont.

David

She pulls a few coins out of her pocket and stands looking at them. He looks in her hand and points to a quarter, a dime, and a nickel saying, "25¢, 35¢, 40¢." She gives him the three coins and takes her books. "Have a nice day," David says. (David has it! Needs more challenging, higher-level, multistep problems.)

Reading Running Records

A reading running record is a formal way to monitor children's reading behaviors by recording exactly what the child does and says while reading (Clay, 1995). In particular, it is a way to learn about the particular reading strategies a child uses to understand the story (e.g., picture or phonetic cues, self-correction, etc.). Reading running records can be used for many purposes, including:

- Documenting behavior for later reflection
- Identifying the reading strategies a child uses
- Determining the child's reading level to help with book selection
- Identifying next instructional steps
- Grouping students
- Monitoring progress
- Making decisions about referrals for additional support or evaluation

There are different ways to document children's behaviors using a reading running record. In some cases, teachers have a copy of the text the child is reading. Or teachers use a code to keep track of exactly what the child reads. When doing reading running records, it is advisable to use a standard coding method that is easily interpreted by others reviewing the documentation. There are several books included under Resources that can help you learn to use this documentation strategy.

Matrices

A matrix or a grid is a way to record a word, a very brief note, or a rating for a few children or for the entire class. Names of students are listed on the left side of the page (or across the top). Space is allocated next to each name for comments. The matrix used by a second-grade teacher to keep track of students' comments during daily literature discussions is shown below. Each day she uses a code to note who participates in the discussion. When she can, she tries to include comments. The class is reading *Stone Fox* by John Gardiner (1996).

Literature Discussions   Week of 3/12 Stone Fox
A - active participation   P - participated somewhat
Q - quiet

Names		Comments/Reflections
Andrew	P	responded to Stevie about Gardiner's motive
Anthony	Q	
Bill	Q	
Collin	A	
Daniel	P	related personal story about being at a farm
Dayshonne	A	noted details about history/ compared to present day
Ebony	P	begins all w/ well, I think... comments not related to topic
Joshua	P	
Katie	Q	recalled details of yesterday's disc.
Keith	P	question about taxes
Lauren	Q	
Leah	P	recalls details; describes Willie's feelings
Matthew	P	
Nadine	Q	Does she get the story? Try to talk to her
Nicole	P	
Richard	P	told personal story about his grandfather
Shawn	P	
Steven	abs	
Trayon	P	

Matrices are also used to focus observations on a set of skills, concepts, or behaviors typically listed across the top of the grid. The following illustration shows how a first-grade teacher kept track of children's skills during a measurement activity. As a result of her observations, she determined that the next step for these children was a measurement activity with a more limited focus.

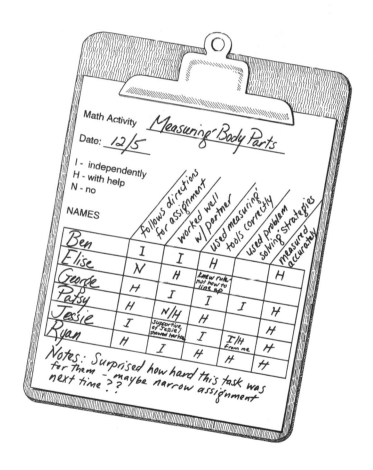

Math Activity Measuring Body Parts

Date: 12/5

I - independently
H - with help
N - no

NAMES

	Follows directions for assignment	worked well w/ partner	Used measuring tools correctly	used problem solving strategies	measured accurately
Ben	I	I	H		
Elise	N	H	knew rule not how to line up		H
George	H	I	I	I	
Patsy	H	N/H	I		H
Jessie	I	Supportive of Jessie showed her how	H		H
Ryan	H	I	I	I/H from me	H
			H	H	H

Notes: Surprised how hard this task was for them — maybe narrow assignment next time??

Rating Scales

Rating scales are intended to show the degree to which children possess a certain skill. The illustration below shows a rating scale used by a kindergarten teacher at the beginning of the year to assess children's knowledge, skills, and participation level during daily opening activities. She includes students' names and a set of skills that she will focus on.

A rating scale allows you to record your observations as events occur. You can quickly record your judgment or evaluation of a child's performance on a particular occasion or as a summary of several observations. Remember that with a rating scale, however, you evaluate a complex behavior in a simple way and, therefore, see only one part of a bigger picture. Rely on other recording methods to capture the subtleties in children's behavior.

N- no P- partial C -competent	days of the week	yesterday/ today/ tomorrow	counting # of days in wk/m.	tens/ ones	recognizes patterns	duplicates /extends patterns
Arletha	P	N				
Austin	C	C	P	P	C	P
Danielle	C	P	??	P	C	C
Dean	P	C	P	P	C	P
Emily	C	C	C	C	C	P
Gyrah	N	ck in w/her			C	C
Kiersten	P	P			P	P
Melissa	C	C	P	P	P	P

Tallies

Tallies are used in two ways: to count the instances of a particular behavior or event and to count the instances of a behavior during a predetermined time interval. The following illustration shows how a preschool teacher used tallies on a matrix to record children's participation during daily group times. This method of recording helped her see patterns of children's involvement in activities. After 2 weeks of recording in this way, she reflected on her observations. She was surprised by how many children participated actively during story time. She decided to do some focused observing in small group situations of the children whose participation was limited during large group times. And, she planned to alter some of the morning circle activities to see if she could elicit greater participation.

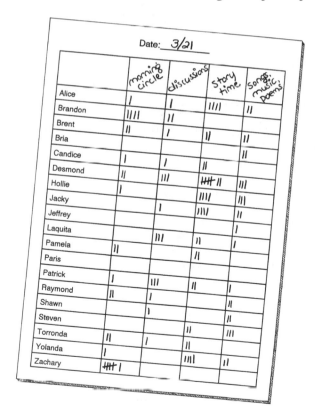

Date: 3/21

	morning circle	discussions	story time	songs; music; poems
Alice	I	I	IIII	II
Brandon	IIII	II		
Brent	II	I		
Bria			II	II
Candice	I	I	II	II
Desmond	II	III		
Hollie	I		HHt II	III
Jacky			IIII	III
Jeffrey		I	IIII	II
Laquita		III	II	I
Pamela	II		II	I
Paris			II	
Patrick	I	III	II	
Raymond	II	I		I
Shawn		I		II
Steven				II
Torronda	II	I	II	III
Yolanda	I		II	
Zachary	HHt I		IIII	II

Diagrams, Sketches, and Photographs

When details of certain activities and projects are needed, photos, sketches, and diagrams may be the best way to capture information. As one teacher said:

> Taking photos helps jog my memory about a specific activity and what each child was doing. When I look at the photo, everything comes flooding back into my head.

It may be much quicker to draw a child's block building than to try to describe it in words. Older students can create these records themselves.

Audiotapes and Videotapes

Audiotapes and videotapes are excellent ways to capture children's language. Skits, puppet shows, storytelling, and reading aloud lend themselves to this method of documentation.

Teachers who observe regularly often use several different recording methods, selecting the method that best fits the particular questions they have and the situation in which they are observing. Equally important is finding a method that feels comfortable and natural.

How Do I Organize the Information I Collect?

If you are going to observe purposefully, you'll need a system that enables you not only to write down what you see but also to make order and learn from the written information you've gathered. Creating a system involves two steps:

1. Record your observations in a way that works for you.

2. Organize and store your written observations so you can go back and learn from them.

Step One: Write Things Down in a Way That Works for You

When you choose tools that fit your needs and personal style, you are much more likely to record your observations. Some caregivers and teachers find jotting brief notes on index cards or sticky notes works for them. Others use a variety of tools, including:

- **Mailing labels.** Attach a sheet of mailing labels to a clipboard. You may want to pre-print them with children's names and the date.

- **Legal pads.** In several key locations, place pads of paper with a pen or pencil attached so they'll always be where you need them.

- **Butcher paper.** Hang butcher paper around the room and make notes directly on the paper or attach sticky notes to it. *Note:* Teachers using this method are not concerned about children or parents reading their notes because they are factual.

- **Masking tape.** Make notes on the tape, tear pieces off, and file in the child's file.

- **Calendars.** Some teachers keep daily notes on a desk calendar. Others have a calendar for each child. Still others post on the wall a large monthly calendar drawn on butcher paper and record notes for themselves and parents of daily highlights.

- **Tape recorders.** Dictate your observations into a tape recorder, but remember that taped information has to be transcribed.

- **Still cameras.** Many teachers find taking a photograph a quick way to capture a record of an event or product.

- **Video cameras.** These are useful tools for documenting children in action.

It may take time to figure out what works for you—be patient during your process of trial and error. Writing down your observations helps you see and reflect on information that you can use to make moment-to-moment decisions, such as: "Should I pick up the rattle and hand it to Josie or let her reach for it herself?" "What can I ask to see whether Renee understands what she just read?" "Who can I have work on the city model with Frank to help him better understand scale?" "How can Jason's parents and I work best together to support his fragile self-esteem?"

Step Two: Organize and Store Your Written Observations So You Can Go Back and Learn From Them

The primary purpose of recording your observations and reviewing them later is to provide you with data for reflection. Teachers describe several different levels of reflection related to observing. The first occurs at the time you observe. Whether you record your observation or not, you act based on what you have seen. Your reflection and your decision about how to respond are almost simultaneous. If, for example, you know that Karla is most likely to bite when she gets in crowded spaces, you immediately steer her in another direction when you observe her heading into the refrigerator box house where two other toddlers are playing.

A second level of reflection occurs when you review your notes at the end of the day or week. Looking over your notes may help you decide to modify your plans for tomorrow or may give you ideas for next week. For example, as Tracy reviews her notes from writer's workshop for the week, she notices that several children have started to include dialogue in their stories. She decides that next week she will focus on dialogue during mini-lessons prior to writer's workshop.

This level of reflection allows you to distance yourself from everyday activities and understand the bigger picture of what is happening in your classroom. You may gain some insight about the pattern of a child's behavior by reviewing your observational notes from several days or a week. Or you may realize something new about your program. For example, after reviewing notes about several children who became involved in fights in the block area, you wonder how to rearrange the furniture to create a more workable space. Taking time to review your notes when you don't have to take immediate action allows you to examine the data more objectively, gain perspective, and make meaning of the information you have collected.

A third level of reflection takes place when you go back and analyze your notes over a longer period of time for purposes of formal assessment—when you need to write a report, prepare for a child study meeting, or conduct a family-teacher conference. This level allows you to recognize progress children have made. It may also show you that troubling behaviors you were worried about 2 months ago have diminished or disappeared.

Review your notes regularly—we recommend weekly, twice a month at the least—to help you get the most from them. For the second and third levels of reflection, organization is essential. Sometimes it sounds easier to review and use information from observation notes than it actually is. Notes have an amazing ability to end up in "black holes"—pockets, filing cabinets, desk drawers—never to be seen again. And when they are sighted, they often tend to be in a state of confusion. During a recent workshop, a brave teacher held up a large jumble of sticky notes all stuck together in a clump. "I can find time to write my observations down," she said. "But I never get back to them." Laughter and a collective sigh of relief swept through the group. Clearly she's not alone. On the next few pages, we provide examples of systems for storing and organizing written observations that teachers, caregivers, and child care providers have shared with us.

I've made a folder for each child in which I keep my observations and notes from other teachers and parents. I'm now in the habit of spending 5 to 10 minutes each week filing my notes.

I use index cards, which I store in a small file box. I create a section for each child. I keep the cards and a pen on the top of the bookshelf so they are handy. I stick the cards in my pocket as I write on them and, at the end of the day, file them under the correct name.

◆　　◆　　◆　　◆　　◆　　◆

I keep a notebook for each baby in my room. Parents are welcome to take their child's book home and add observations from home. It works very well.

◆　　◆　　◆　　◆　　◆　　◆

We have portfolios for each child that I made out of an accordion folder. In each portfolio, we keep observations and samples of that child's work that are shared with the child and his or her family. The child helps us choose which pieces of work to include. I keep my scribbled observations in a folder labeled with that child's name and stored in my filing cabinet.

◆　◆　◆　◆　◆　◆

I hung a shoe bag in one of the closets of my family child care home. I label a section for each child and keep my notes about him or her right there.

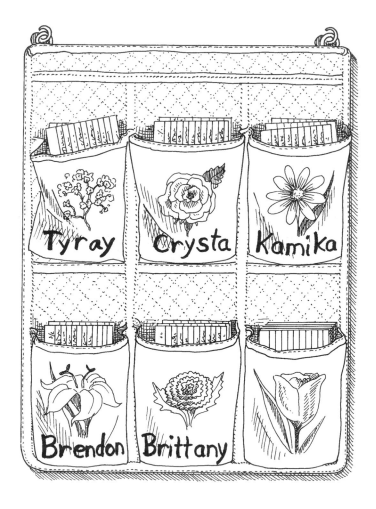

In addition to your notes on individual children, think about how to store the observations you record on rating scales, matrices, and tallies used when working with a group. This is especially important if you work with children who are pre-school age and older. Many teachers find it helpful to keep a three-ring binder for these tools, which they organize by subject area. They then thumb through it as they reflect on individual children.

As you review your current system or consider what kind of system to develop, be sure it works for you. It should be convenient and easy to use. There should always be something to write with and on close at hand. Putting away your observations should be a simple task whether you do it when children are resting or out at music, at the end of each day, or at the end of the week. As you put away your notes, take a moment to scan them. If a question jumps out, jot it down in your plans to remind you about something you want to observe. Beware if you find a bunch of random notes growing in the corner: This is a sign that something is not working. Modify your system, if necessary, to keep your system from overwhelming you.

In the end, only two things about your system really count: Do you use your system? Does it help you better understand and respond to the children and families with whom you work?

SUMMING UP

Effective observing is an ongoing process of asking questions and making decisions. If you are aware of these questions and think about them ahead of time, you will increase your chances of finding out what you want to know about children, families, and yourself as a teacher:

- **What do I want to find out?** Putting what you want to learn into a question provides you with a clear purpose as an observer and often makes observing a richer, more gratifying experience.

- **When and where should I observe to get the information I want?** There will be times when you observe because you see or hear something that strikes you as curious or simply because you have a free moment. There will be other times when observing is planned rather than spontaneous.

- **How do I record what I observe?** There are many ways to record observational data, including brief notes, anecdotal notes, running records, rating scales, matrices, tallies, diagrams, sketches, and photographs. The method you use depends on what you want to learn, the activities children are engaged in, your responsibilities when you are observing, and your personal style.

- **How am I going to organize the information I collect?** As a purposeful observer, you need a system that enables you to write down what you see and allows you to make order and learn from the written information you gather. Creating a system involves two steps: one, write things down in a way that works for you, and two, organize and store your written information so you can go back and learn from it.

In chapter 6, we examine how you apply the information you collect to the many decisions you make each day in your classroom.

Using What You Learn

Throughout this book, you have read about teachers who use what they learn by observing to promote positive relationships and support children's learning. In this chapter, we highlight specific ways to use what you learn to make your program responsive to children, to respond to individuals and the group, to conduct assessments and report information, and to work effectively with families. We begin by revisiting the practice of observation, which is an ongoing cycle of asking questions; watching, listening, and taking notes; reflecting; and responding.

Revisiting the Practice of Observation

When you observe, you gain insights about children's strengths, knowledge, interests, and skills. You may also discover barriers to children's learning. Observation begins with your wondering about a child and asking questions about

his or her behavior. You collect data and then reflect on what you have learned. You interpret what the child did and said, and you respond on the basis of that interpretation. Sometimes you find that your interpretation makes sense; sometimes it does not. You often find that you need more information, so you ask new questions. Observation is an ongoing cycle.

Wonder and Ask Questions

Observation begins with your willingness to learn about children and about your practice. It starts with a question about a child. The question might be as simple as "How can I get to know this child?" or "What materials can I add to the science area to engage children's interests?" Your purpose for observing is to answer your question, and your question determines where, when, and how to observe.

For example, if you want to observe Jimmy's language skills to complete an assessment and prepare for an upcoming conference with his family, you might observe during small-group activities, snack time, and perhaps choice time. You would jot notes during those times to capture accurate samples of his language. If you wanted to observe his gross motor skills, you wouldn't observe during snack time but would instead take your pad and pencil with you to observe Jimmy during outdoor choice time or on a class walk to the park.

Watch, Listen, and Take Notes

Observation is an integral part of everyday teaching. You can do it anywhere and anytime: while you are part of the action, while you are out of the action, or after the action. Writing notes about what you see and hear, taking photographs, and collecting work samples provide meaningful documentation that helps you remember your observations and think about them as you plan. Observing and comparing notes with colleagues and family members also help you pay attention to things you might have missed if you were working alone.

Reflect

Pausing to think about your observations is an essential phase in the cycle, so reflection must not be hurried or overlooked. It is critical to making meaningful decisions about children's learning and development.

As you review recent observations, ask yourself, "What is going on and what does this information tell me about how can I support this child?" An on-the-spot reflection can help you adjust your interaction with a child so that it meets that child's immediate needs. Reflecting as you plan leads you to design or adapt activities so that they match children's developmental levels and interests. Information from observing and reflecting gives you clues about what children are ready to learn and how they can learn it. As you reflect on what you see and hear, you try to form a possible explanation of the child's behavior. You will know if your idea is right only after you respond to the child and determine the effect of your response.

Here are some questions to ask yourself as you consider the meaning of the behavior you documented:

- What's going on here? What is the child experiencing?
- What does this tell me about
    - this child as an individual?
    - the child's skills and knowledge?
    - how the child approaches learning?
- How can I use this information to build a better relationship with this child?
- How do I use this information to stretch a child's thinking, understanding, knowledge, and skills?
- Does the child need me to step back and give her time and space? Does she need my assistance? If so, how much and what kind of assistance does she need?
- What can I do to sustain a child's excitement, learning, and sense of competence?

Respond

The data you collect by observing is only meaningful when it is linked to decisions about teaching. Every decision you make affects children's learning.

Sometimes your decisions about how to respond are almost automatic. You wonder about something a child is doing, watch and listen briefly, quickly form a possible explanation of the behaviors you see, and decide how to respond a moment later. In other instances, you are more deliberate. You have a question, so you plan how and when to observe. Then, at a later time and perhaps with a supervisor, another teacher, or family members, you reflect on the child's behavioral patterns, interpret the child's behavior, and plan your response.

In the pages that follow, you will see examples of how teachers use the observation cycle to respond in a variety of ways. The stories show how the knowledge and insights teachers gain by observing help them

- Make their program responsive to children
- Respond to individuals and the group
- Conduct assessments and create reports
- Work together with families

We have used a variety of formats to present the stories in this chapter. Short examples illustrate specific points. Longer, more detailed stories demonstrate different phases of the observation cycle. The consistent feature of the stories is how observation strengthens relationships and promotes children's success as learners.

Making Your Program Responsive to Children

Observation often helps caregivers and teachers adapt the environment and shape daily routines to be more responsive to children's strengths and needs. As you read these examples, reflect on your own setting, what you observe there, and modifications you could make to support the children you work with each day.

Adapting the Environment

Observation gives you insights about how children use the environment. You can use this information to change the environment to promote children's exploration, interactions, and learning. Consider the examples that follow.

In an infant-toddler program:
At the end of the day, Karlene, an infant caregiver, reflects on what she saw during the past week.

> Over the past 3 days, Lynn, age 7 months, has been getting up on her hands and knees and rocking back and forth. Today, she put one hand in front of the other, moved a knee forward, rocked slightly back, and then crawled for several feet. She is the first child in our group to begin crawling.

As a result of this observation, Karlene decides to be extra careful about safety. She explains,

> Although we are always mindful of safety, the situation is different now that we have a child who crawls. I will crawl around the floor tomorrow and look again for hazards. Once we solve any problems, we'll be able to let Lynn explore the room freely.

In a kindergarten classroom:

After observing more frequent disputes in the dramatic play area, Leona, a kindergarten teacher, stepped back and watched for a few minutes. She saw that children were arguing over who could wear the hats and work gloves similar to those their parents wear while working in the fields.

In response, she enlarged the area and included more clothing props. She asked families to bring in one or two of the cardboard crates that are used for storing the broccoli that was being harvested in the fields. After she changed the area, the children expanded their play to include delivering the broccoli to the store. With more space and props, the children's engagement increased and the number of conflicts diminished.

In a primary classroom:

Richard, a teacher of 6- and 7-year-olds, recently observed that children were entering the art area but leaving it almost immediately. Even Carla and Ben, who love to paint, left right away. When he looked at the art area carefully, he saw containers of dried paint and shelves crammed with trays, paper, and brushes. He also realized that one of the easels had been transformed into a private nook for reading. He commented,

> I was surprised and a little embarrassed about how messy things had gotten. No wonder the children didn't want to paint! Rather than handling it myself, I decided to present the children with a problem-solving task. This morning during meeting time, we looked at the art area together and made a plan to straighten it out. I predict that it will be back in full use by next week.

Shaping Daily Routines

For children, one of the best things about daily routines is that they occur every day and often several times a day. Because they also take place at home, routines are natural connections between children's homes and the program. In addition, they are predictable enough to give children a sense of order. As children develop, routines offer new challenges and take on new meaning. Observing periodically during routines will help you give these daily events the same attention and planning as all of the other valuable learning activities in your program.

In an infant-toddler program:
A teacher of toddlers observed Ella during hellos and good-byes in an attempt to figure out how to make transitions easier for the 2-year-old. One of his observations, recorded later, reads,

6/22, Morning arrival

Ella and father hold hands as they walk into room and to table with puzzles. Father sits at table; E climbs into chair. F picks up 3 puzzles pieces; hands piece to E. E pushes his hand away; says, "No!" F hands her second piece; E pushes hand away again; says, "No!" F hands E third piece; E pushes hand away again; says, "No!" E pushes rest of pieces onto floor; says, "No!" Two minutes later, F says, "Okay, Ella, I am going to go to work now." E says, "No!"

A few weeks later, the teacher made the following notes in Ella's book:

7/14, Morning arrival

Ella and father walk into room holding hands. Walk to library area. F: "Ella, let's read a book before I leave today." I join them in library area and suggest that E choose book. E walks to bookshelf, smiles at F, turns back to shelf, takes <u>Very Hungry Caterpillar</u> off shelf, walks back to F, smiles. E sits on F's lap as they look through book. Finish reading; E returns book to shelf. F: "Okay, Ella, it is time for me to go to work now." I walk over to E; ask, "Would you like to walk daddy to the door, or would you like to wave to him from the window?" E: "Go to door." The 3 of us walk to door. F bends down; E opens her arms to give him hug; says, "Bye-bye."

Reading through his notes, the teacher noticed that Ella seems to manage better when she has some control over what is going on. He wondered if establishing a good-bye ritual and giving her realistic choices would help her feel a little more in control of separations and reunions. The next day, he talked with his co-teacher. They agreed to talk with her father about how he can continue to include Ella in making choices when they are saying hello and good-bye to each other. They will also give her manageable choices during the morning and throughout the day.

In a preschool program:

Linda, a preschool teacher, observed that rest time was getting to be a struggle, especially with Nicholas, age 4 years. She wants to answer the question, "What makes rest time so challenging for Nicholas?" To find the answer, Linda decides to observe him at rest time over the course of the week. At the end of the week, she reviewed her notes.

Monday, 10/3

When I dim the lights and say, " It is time for a rest," Nicholas stands next to his mat and says, " I don't want to rest."

Tuesday, 10/4

When I dim the lights and say, " It is time for a rest," Nicholas lies on his mat for 2 minutes. Then he laughs and rolls off his mat and onto his neighbor's mat, waking her up.

Wednesday, 10/5

When I dim the lights and say, " It is time for a rest," Nicholas says, " I don't want to sleep. I want to play," and he runs to the block area.

Thursday, 10/6

When I dim the lights and say, " It is time for a rest," Nicholas lies down on his mat for 5 minutes. Then he gets up and walks to the toys and games area, saying, " I don't want to rest."

Friday, 10/7

When I dim the lights and say, " It is time for a rest," Nicholas says, " I'm not tired. I want to play."

Then Linda uses what she learned by observing to come up with a plan: She will adapt rest time by letting Nicholas—and other children who don't sleep or nap—bring items for a quiet activity to their mats, such as paper, crayons, and books.

Her observation note from Monday stated,

On 10/10, I said, "It is time for a rest. You may take an item from the basket to your mat, to play with quietly during rest time." Nicholas chose a basket of crayons and some paper and walked back to his mat. He got on his mat and began to draw. He stayed on his mat during the entire rest time.

In a third-grade classroom:
Over the last month, Pauline observed that her students were restless during large-group time. They began to have side conversations, take materials off of the neighboring shelves, and leave the group to go to the bathroom or put something in their cubbies. In response, she decided to discuss their restlessness with the class. As a group, they decided to try to solve the problem by changing meeting seats each week.

After 2 weeks, Pauline asked the children if they had observed a difference in group meeting behavior. They agreed that the situation had improved. To herself, Pauline noted that giving the students a chance to think about and try to solve the problem helped them become more conscious of their behavior.

Responding to Individuals and the Group

Whether observing an individual or a group, your response will depend on the situation. Take a deep breath and enjoy those moments when you may step back, observe, appreciate, and enjoy what you see. Always be ready to step in if needed, but, more times than not, a little waiting can help you decide just the right way to respond. You may choose to intervene to strengthen relationships among children or because they are ready to learn a new skill. Sometimes your responses are immediate; others are deferred.

You might be asking, "But what exactly should I do on the basis of my observations?" The answer is to use what you know about a child or children to think about the kind of intervention that will work best.

Depending on the child's individual characteristics and the situation, there are many possibilities:

- **Just listen.** For example, stop what you are doing to pay close attention as Carlos tells you about the fire engine he saw on the way to school.

- **Acknowledge what you see, verbally or with a gesture or facial expression.** For example, your glance will let the five children working in the science center know it is time to quiet down and focus on comparing the weights of the objects you have set out on the table.

- **Share a child's pleasure in a discovery.** For example, pausing to smile and share Wini's excitement about the ants she sees in the play yard encourages her to keep exploring.

- **Use open-ended prompts to extend thinking.**
  Remember, open-ended questions have many
  answers and often begin in these ways: "How did
  you…?", "Why do you think …?", "What would happen
  if …?", and "How would you feel if …?" Another open-
  ended prompt begins with the phrase "Tell me more
  about…"

- **Redirect behavior.** For example, invite a mobile
  infant who has been knocking down other children's
  blocks to read with you.

- **Offer other materials to extend the child's
  thinking.** For example, Joey, a second grader,
  draws and writes about spaceships almost every
  day. To build on his interest and extend his
  learning, you might invite him to work with you
  at the computer to look at the NASA Web site,
  where he can see pictures of space shuttles.
  Together you can talk about what shuttles look like
  and how they are designed.

- **Model a new skill.** For example, show Tina how to
  use her thumb and first finger to close the snaps on
  her jacket.

- **Offer information and instruction.** For example,
  read and discuss the steps in the recipe before
  beginning to make pretzels with a group of first
  graders.

- **Create or add challenge.** For example, ask children
  to estimate and figure out how to measure the length
  of the school building.

In the stories below, you will see how teachers step in to support
individual children, extend children's learning, respond to the
group, and balance group and individual needs.

Supporting Individual Children

Children, like all of us, learn best when they have trusting relationships with their teachers and when what they are learning is meaningful to them. In the stories below, teachers use what they know about children to strengthen their relationships and shape instruction on the basis of the strengths, interests, and needs of each child.

Helping a Child Feel Safe and Secure

When Korene's primary caregiver observes that Korene, age 7 months, smiles and kicks her legs whenever she hears music, she decides to ask Korene's parents about the music they listen to at home. When they offer to bring in some jazz tapes, she enthusiastically encourages them to do so. She makes a point of listening to and enjoying Korene's family's favorite music with Korene and the other children, to help Korene feel comfortable in child care.

Following a Child's Interests to Build a Relationship

A preschool teacher noted her observations about Larisa, age 3, on an index card. Larisa's home language is Russian, and she is in the nonverbal stage of English-language learning. This is what the teacher wrote:

9/17—We talked about pets during circle time. Larisa did not participate in discussion verbally. 9/18—L and her mother brought pet guinea pig to school.

The teacher explains:

> I discovered that Larisa understands more English than I had
> originally thought. I realized that I needed to help Larisa feel safe
> enough to begin speaking English. I have a camera in the classroom,
> so I took some photos of Larisa; her mom; and Tiger, the guinea pig.
> I gave one photo to Larisa to take home and kept some in our class
> photo album to remind Larisa and the other children of the special
> day when Tiger came to school. Using the pictures we took, Larisa
> and I wrote a story about Tiger. Larisa drew the illustrations, and I
> wrote simple captions in English that she understands.

Shaping Instruction on the Basis of a Child's Culture

Leslie, a first-grade teacher in rural New England, overheard two
children imitating the accent of a new child who is Vietnamese.
She realized that, living where they do, most of her children's
exposure to different ethnic and cultural groups is very limited.
She knows that it is important for them to learn more about
various groups of people who live in the United States and across
the world. She plans to bring in music, books, and photos of and
about different cultures. She will also begin the study of families
that she had originally planned for later in the year. As children
discuss their families, she will highlight differences and similarities
among them. An important part of the study will be to involve
the children's families in planning and implementing learning
activities and in celebrating what the children learn.

Extending Children's Learning

Young children are learning all the time, and they benefit from
your guidance. You can help them think about something
differently, ask new questions, and learn new skills. In the stories
below, notice the strategies that the teachers, Mr. Seiko and
Ms. Geiger, use.

In a preschool classroom:

Maya is an English-language learner whose home language is Spanish, but Mr. Seiko knows only a few Spanish words. This week, Mr. Seiko focuses on two learning goals for Maya, a 4-year-old in his preschool classroom: 1) interacting with peers and adults and 2) using language to express ideas in her home language and in English. His observations are guided by his questions about her language skills.

10/25

3 children in block area. R and S build structure together. Maya builds independently; places 3 long flat blocks side by side. No verbal exchange between Maya and other children.

10/29

Maya sorts magnetic letters by color; places them in rows on table. T: "Maya, I see you are sorting the letters." M smiles. T: "How are you sorting them?" M continues to sort. T: "It looks like you are sorting them by color." M smiles, hands blue letter B, points to row of blue letters.

11/3

Maya in block area, building independently. Uses 10 blocks to make enclosure; then puts cars inside.

As he reflects on his recent observations of Maya, he notes that she usually chooses the block area and toys and games area at choice time, playing quietly by herself.

Mr. Seiko decides that he will spend a few minutes working with Maya on Monday during choice time. After she has gone to the block area, he joins the four children who are playing in the area. Two children, Savannah and Tyrone, are building a tall structure together. Robert has made a road and is driving a car on it. Maya has lined up several long blocks along the edge of the block shelves.

After sitting with the children and observing for a few moments, Mr. Seiko says to Maya, "I see you used 10 blocks that are all the same size." She looks up at him. Turning to Robert, who is able to use English and Spanish, Mr. Seiko says, "Shall we ask Maya if she wants to connect her structure to your road? It would be much longer that way. The car could travel farther." Robert begins to connect the two structures, not speaking. Mr. Seiko encourages, "Check with Maya to see if it is okay. Ask her in Spanish." As Robert begins to speak to Maya in Spanish, she nods her head, says, "Sí," and adds a connecting block. Mr. Seiko says, "Maya, I see you are connecting the roads." At the end of the day Mr. Seiko adds a few books about roads and bridges to the block area. He will show them to Maya and Robert in the morning before choice time.

In a first-grade classroom:
Ms. Geiger recently reviewed her observation notes and other written records related to the learning goal "Students will self-select appropriate texts for a variety of purposes." In order to keep track of children's progress toward this goal, she marks a class list during quiet reading and choice times, when children tell her about a book they are reading, when she reads with them, or when they complete a file card in the reading box. She noticed that Kenny did not have any tally marks next to his name.

She considers what she has learned about Kenny. She knows that he excels at soccer but does not like to read. His mom has reported that, when she asks him to read for 20 minutes each day at home, she often finds him building a hideout for his pet rabbit with the books in his bedroom.

On the basis of her observations and reflections, Ms. Geiger decides how to respond. In an effort to encourage his reading, she will find some books and magazines about soccer and rabbits to give to Kenny. She will also find a book with very simple text about children his age.

Responding to the Group

Responding to the group requires thoughtful planning and, at the same time, a willingness to modify your plans according to the needs of the group. In the stories below, the teachers observe their children carefully. This gives them the information they need to adjust their plans according to the group's mood and dynamics, interests, knowledge, and skills.

Adjusting Plans According to the Group's Mood and Dynamics

For the last 2 days, Lanice has noticed more crying, grabbing, and hitting in her mixed-age infant-toddler room. The next morning, she mentions her observations to her co-teacher, Eugene. He comments "I'm glad you said something. I noticed the same thing." They wonder why the children are irritable and decide quickly to review what they know about each child.

As they gather supplies for a planned finger-painting experience, they think about each child. They remember that Kari's father is about to be deployed by the military, that her family is trying to prepare for his being away for at least 6 to 8 months, and that Kari usually has a hard time managing change. They also think about the fact that Shalish's grandparents have just arrived from India to stay with his family. Jesse has a cold, and she can't sleep when her nose is stuffed.

Lanice realizes, "We were so busy, we missed the fact that two of our eight kids have big changes going on in their lives, and one of them has a cold. I think all of that is changing the dynamics of the whole group." Eugene agrees.

They look at the three containers of paint. Lanice asks, "Remember how everyone got covered in paint last time and we had to spend an hour wiping paint off children, the floor, and us?"

Eugene responds, "I know we can manage painting experiences better, but the children need extra attention now. We should rearrange our plans according to the children's emotional needs and what we learned this morning. Let's do something less messy today so we can interact more easily with the children."

Lanice agrees, "You're right. Why don't we pack up the blanket, balls, and bubbles and go to the park for a morning of playing and talking together? Maybe that will help the children adjust to the changes."

Adjusting Plans According to the Group's Interests

The children in Ms. Leffert's kindergarten class are studying buildings. After a group discussion about the different types of buildings they are likely to see on a walk near school, they leave the school with clipboards and pencils to draw and write about what they observe. As they turn the corner onto the main street, several of the children stop to watch a construction site.

At first, Ms. Leffert encourages them to keep walking down the street. Hearing the excited conversation of the children as they watch the huge trucks and other machinery at the site, she decides to wait. About 3 minutes later, the big crane that is lifting metal beams captures everyone's attention. Letting go of her initial plans, she asks the children, "Shall we stay and watch the construction?" All hands fly up, accompanied by cheers. She suggests that the children sketch their observations of the construction site.

Ms. Leffert uses her observations of the group to shift the purpose of the class's walk for two reasons: She wants to build on the children's interest and excitement about the construction site, and she knows that she can help children reach the same learning goals by pursuing this slightly different topic. Back in the classroom, the group gathers in the meeting area to talk about their experience. Ms. Leffert begins the discussion by saying, "Wow! We sure saw many different kinds of construction materials. Let's make a list." She begins listing their ideas on the chart titled, "Materials at the Construction Site."

Adjusting Plans According to the Group's Knowledge and Skills

Teachers often plan lessons for a small group or for the whole class when they think that children are ready to learn a skill. Ms. Perez's story about her third graders illustrates the importance of using immediate observation to adjust lesson plans.

Following my district and state math standards, I planned a lesson related to quantity and based on an activity I heard about at a workshop. Each child was to write a numeral between 100 and 1,000 on an index card. I strung a clothesline across the classroom and put a card with the numeral *100* on the left and a card with *1,000* on the right. Children were to work together to hang their numerals in the correct order from 100 to 1,000. However, the children were not ready for this activity. The cards were placed in the wrong order, and the children disagreed about what they were supposed to do and how to do it.

I changed my approach immediately. I asked the children to stop what they were doing and sit on the rug. Together, we ordered the numeral cards between 100 and 200. It was a great opportunity for me to observe children's misunderstandings about three-digit numbers. We decided that we would do the activity differently and extend it over several days. We hung the six numeral cards we had between 100 and 200 on the line in the correct order. Then we agreed that we would focus next on numbers between 200 and 300.

Balancing Individual and Group Needs

Creating a community of learners with children who are diverse in temperament, family and cultural backgrounds, interests, and skills is a perpetual juggling act. It requires teachers to pay attention to the whole group as well as to observe each child. In the stories below, teachers plan for a group of children with diverse skills and knowledge. They also respond to challenging behavior in order to protect the functioning of the group while ensuring that each child has positive learning experiences. In the final story, a teacher enlists the help of a colleague to make sense of her perceptions. That enables her to relax, observe individual children and the group objectively, and respond effectively.

Planning for a Group With Diverse Skills and Abilities

Mr. Adams plans small-group activities in his preschool classroom by using information from his observations to decide learning goals; groups; and how to offer learning experiences that meet children's strengths, interests, and needs. Here is his story about planning a small-group lesson for children with diverse skills.

> Over the past few weeks, I have observed many children using the discovery area. A variety of natural materials are displayed there, including rocks, a bowl of sand, a bin of soil, and a collection of branches. The children are already engaged with observing and describing the materials, so I thought that introducing the balance scale would encourage them to explore weight and balance.
>
> I considered the varying skills and interests of four children as I planned a small-group activity. Carlos chooses different interest areas in the classroom, uses complex sentences, and brings books into the interest areas. Daniella uses new information, new vocabulary, and complex sentences. Rick chooses the discovery area 3–4 times a week, uses simple sentences of 3–4 words, and is being evaluated by a speech and language therapist. Tanika includes many details when she retells stories or events, chooses the discovery area 2–3 times a week, and engages in elaborate and sustained dramatic play.

The primary goal for this lesson was to introduce the balance scale. I wanted to explain its name and purpose, show children how to handle it, and encourage them to think about ways they might use it to explore materials. By keeping the lesson open-ended and relying on their cues, I kept the children's interest and engagement high.

When the children came into the discovery area, the balance scale was already on the table. The children immediately noticed and began to examine it. From time to time, I keep a running record of children's language during small groups because it gives me a lot of anecdotal information. Here's the record:

I: *I'm writing down what we say so that we have a record of it. (They look at my clipboard and go back to examining the scale.)*

Tanika: *I'll put rocks in. (She places a large rock in the right side, and the scale tips. All of the children giggle.)*

Carlos: *Look what happened, Tanika. You broke it!*

Tanika: *No, I didn't. (She takes her big rock out, and the scale balances. More giggles.)*

Carlos: *I'll put these little ones in. (He puts two small stones on one side, and each child adds stones to the other side.)*

I: *What happens when you put stones in the cups?*

Daniella: *The cups tip. Is it just for rocks?*

I: *Daniella, why do you think it might only be for rocks?*

Daniella: *Dunno.*

I: *This is called a balance scale. You can use it to weigh many things. Have any of you seen one of these before? (I turn to Ricky.) Have you seen one?*

Ricky:	(Shrugs and puts small stones in the cup.)
Tanika:	Like in dramatic play. We got one in there.
Daniella:	There's a big scale at my doctor's office.
Carlos:	Mine, too.
I:	That's right. Those are all scales. Do you know what those scales are used for?
Carlos:	To get weighed. I weigh four.
I:	Carlos. Tell us why you think you weigh four.
Carlos:	Dunno.
I:	Scales measure weight, or how heavy things are. This scale can help us learn about the weight of the objects on our discovery table. Shall we do some investigating? (All of the children nod, "Yes.") Since we started experimenting with the rocks, let's keep going. (More nods.) Ricky, "Finish filling this cup with the small stones." (Ricky adds three more and stops.)
I:	What happened, Ricky?
Ricky:	Gestures with his hand that the cup went down.
I:	That's right, Ricky. This cup moved down. Why do you think that happened?
Ricky:	(Smiles and points to the cup again.)

After encouraging the children to explore the balance scale for another 5 minutes, I suggested that we write down some of our observations.

Here is what we wrote.

What We Noticed About the Balance Scale

Tanika: The gray rock makes the cup go down more. The side with the black rock stays up.

Carlos: Two little rocks in one bucket and two little rocks in the other bucket. The buckets stay the same.

Daniella: When we put all the rocks in one cup but none in the other, it tips all over.

Ricky noticed that the cup with more rocks tipped more.

Reflection

In addition to the overall learning goals for this activity, I considered more questions as I watched the children work. I asked myself, "What are my goals for individual children?" I wanted Ricky to feel like part of the group, to express his ideas even without oral English skills, and to hear language related to measurement. Carlos is very quick to talk and act, but I also wanted him to listen to the other children's ideas. As children made observations, I switched from the running record to writing on a chart so their ideas can be displayed in the discovery area to prompt other children's thinking and expression. I also wanted Ricky to see his name on the observation chart. Daniella and Tanika had the great idea of illustrating the chart. I hadn't thought of that.

All of the children had some prior knowledge about scales, but they also had misconceptions. I wanted them to share their ideas with each other. By the end of the 15-minute lesson, I had introduced several new words and concepts: *balance, more, less, the same, weight, balance scale.* The children used the balance scale to compare the weight of rocks.

Next steps

I will use the chart this group of children made with the rest of the small groups when I am introducing the scale to them. I will also encourage the next small group to draw and write about what they notice during their balance scale investigations.

Responding to Challenging Behavior

Many caring teachers struggle to deal with the challenging behaviors of children in their classrooms. The following two stories show how information gathered through observation helped teachers to understand better a child's behavior and how they could respond to foster that child's competence while meeting the needs of the group.

In an infant-toddler program:

At the end of the day, Sharon tells her supervisor, Mrs. Green, "Karla, who is 13 months old now, bit two kids on Monday. I've never known her to bite. Today we changed our plans for making pancakes, which everyone loves, so I could shadow her. Steve and Audrey wanted me to read with them, but I had to keep my eye on Karla. The group is giving up learning opportunities because of one child. That is hard for Karla, too."

"Are any other new things going on in your room?" asks Ms. Green.

"At the last minute, Maria had to be out this week to take care of her mother," explains Sharon, "but the children know and like the substitute. We met early Monday morning to plan. She's easy to work with. I don't think she is the problem."

Ms. Green suggests, "Let's use your observations to answer the question: 'What's going on with Karla?' Here, let's look through some of the observation notes you made about her last month."

3/26

Snack time—K climbs into chair next to Maria. K picks up cracker with right hand, takes bite, puts cracker down, picks up sippy cup with both hands, drinks. Puts cup down; touches M's sleeve. M looks down; asks, "It's nice to sit together and eat snack, isn't it? Do you want a slice of banana?" K smiles; answers, "'Nana." K reaches for slice; eats it.

3/29

Choice time—K pulls book off shelf; carries it across room to Maria. M: "Do you want to read this book together?" K smiles; nods head up and down.

3/30

Arrival time—K's mother adds snap bead to chain they are making; says, "I have to go to work now. I'll come back after your nap like I always do. Sharon will help you today." As mother puts her coat on, K pulls mother's skirt; says, "Pick up." I kneel and explain that her mommy will come back. Mother nods at me. I pick K up; we walk M to door and wave good-bye. K squirms. I put her down. She sits in corner; sucks thumb. I go to her. Head down, she turns her body toward wall, away from me. Maria walks in. K looks and reaches her arms toward Maria.

Reflection

Reviewing last month's observations helped Sharon remember something about Karla that she had not considered at first. She formed a thoughtful guess about Karla's biting and explained,

> Karla arrived late on Monday morning, after I told the children that Maria was going to be away for the week. Karla has a very trusting relationship with Maria, and I forgot to explain Maria's absence to her. Karla is reserved, and it is hard at first for her to let me help her. I think she may be upset and confused about where Maria is, and that might be why she is biting.

Next steps

First thing in the morning, Sharon is going to reinforce Karla's connection with Maria to try to help Karla feel safe and more comfortable while Maria is gone. She will explain that Maria is away and assure her that Maria will come back. She will hang Maria's picture on the refrigerator and talk about Maria during the day. For example, at snack time she will talk about the time the children made applesauce with Maria.

Sharon is also going to keep a close watch on Karla, try to prevent upsetting situations, and offer activities that Karla enjoys. She will also plan ways to give Karla time away from the large group as necessary, for example, by dividing into small groups for a neighborhood walk and by asking Karla and the substitute teacher to go to the kitchen for pancake ingredients.

At the same time, she is going to plan for the group. For example, she will explain her new insights about Karla's biting to the substitute, and together they will plan ways to help Karla manage her feelings and behavior.

In a second-grade classroom:

Jolene, a teacher in an urban public school, has 29 children in her second-grade classroom. An excellent classroom manager and usually quite resourceful in finding ways to support children, Jolene was concerned about Denise's behavior. She thought it interfered with the learning of both Denise and the group, but she didn't know how to respond. She explained,

> Denise joined our class a few weeks into the school year. I have found that, when I talk with her one-to-one, she converses well and shares her ideas. When I'm teaching a lesson, though, she doesn't seem to understand what is going on. She doesn't follow directions. She moves around during discussions and can only focus on a task for a minute or two. I'm continually telling her to return to her seat, to keep her hands to herself, and to wait until small-group time to talk to friends.

One day, as a student teacher was conducting a whole-group math lesson, Jolene stepped out of the action to observe. She wanted more information in order to answer some of her questions about Denise: What does Denise do? Does her behavior interfere with her learning? Does her behavior interfere with the group? Jolene observed and recorded the following running record:

9/26

9:00 a.m.—D is sitting at her desk, lifts pile of papers and books, searches for math book and calculator. She takes out old spelling test, looks it over. Looks at me. Gets up, walks to me, asks me to show her what book to use. I do. D returns to seat. Finds her calculator. Child sitting next to her gives her book from absent student's desk.

Directions given. D looks around. Ms. P helps her begin solving problem; D completes problem by self. Group discussion begins. D raises hand to answer question; calls, "Ooooo." Kneels on chair, looks at books of two girls across from her, lies across desk, nudges S, tells her to look at her completed page. Enters 42 on calculator; asks S, "Minus?" Pushes buttons before more directions are given. Clears calculator. Kneels; holds hand up; calls out, "Fifty." Points to problem on page in her book. Kneels; looks at R's book; yells, "Fifty"; writes answer in her notebook.

Looks around room. To R, "Ain't we right here?" Enters 108 on calculator. Kneels, turns around, looks at book, looks at board, talks to no one in particular, smiles. Looks at other children's books. Says to self, "Oh, it's twenty." Erases answer. Picks up calculator; says, "Oh, it's twenty," again. Punches numbers on calculator. Looks at numbers on board; says, "Oh," and enters 584 on calculator. K tells her it is the wrong number. D doesn't respond. Enters the wrong numbers while oral directions given. After correct numbers are written on board, D clears calculator and enters them. Keeps looking from board to book. Looks at each number on board and enters it. Says, "Man, ain't this the answer?" Rocks on knees, leans across the desk, asks others what to do next. Says, "804 take away," and bangs on calculator. Closes calculator and book when asked to do so.

Reflection

Jolene observed things that she was not able to see when she was directing the action of the class. She explains,

> I was able to see that Denise was actually on task much of the time. When I'm teaching and she's moving around, my perception is that she's just fooling around. It really bothers me.

> After watching her, I realize that her movement seems to be part of her way of keeping herself on task and of getting the right answer. She's trying to solve the math problem, but she's not really sure how to do that. She doesn't seem to understand the oral directions. As I watched her, I got the sense that she really wants to do what the other children are doing, but she doesn't know how to proceed. She needs to have each step of the problem solving process and each step of calculator use explained.

> I also used to think that she was distracting the other children with all of her movement and talking. Now I see that I was the only person who was distracted. Denise wants the children to help her with the answer or to know on what step of the process she should be. They aren't bothered by her behavior at all.

Next steps

This observation provided Jolene with several new ideas about how to support Denise. She decided to ignore some of her talking and moving. Instead of saying, "Denise, are you talking again?" she now gives a silent, visual clue to help Denise understand what to do next. For example, she might point to a number or word on a page to help her find her place.

Jolene talked to Denise about her observation. When she asked Denise if she was having trouble understanding what to do, Denise said, "Yes." Jolene also suggested that Denise sit next to Shawnesse, who can help her understand each step of the task. That way, Denise will not have talk to more than one child. Denise responded very positively to the suggestion. Jolene reported, "Denise smiled at the end of our conversation."

After observing Denise, Jolene now has new questions about her:

- Why doesn't she understand oral directions?

- What would help her? A peer partner? My speaking more slowly? Using more visual cues?

- What would keep her from becoming frustrated so easily? Would it help to show her each step of the task?

- Does she have a hearing or auditory processing problem? Has she ever been tested for any physical or learning problems?

Jolene will continue to observe and look for answers to these and other questions that arise.

Balancing Your Perceptions of Individuals and Groups

Pamela, a third-grade teacher, tells a story about Ben, an 8-year-old diagnosed with attention-deficit/hyperactivity disorder. It shows how a teacher's perspective affects the balance between the needs of individuals and the group.

> My attention was always focused on Ben—or at least I thought it needed to be. Despite how challenging his behavior was to manage, I really enjoyed teaching him. He has the most wonderful smile and a great sense of humor. I sensed that he is smart. When we talked one-on-one, he was able to express his thoughts verbally. If I was able to spend extended periods of time with him, he surprised me with his insights. During group time, he tried endlessly to share his ideas, but he rarely expressed them clearly.

His arrival in the classroom each day was like a tornado. He would charge through the door and bump into a cabinet or bookcase. He attempted to hang up his coat and backpack, but he usually flung them at the hooks, so they landed on the floor. Each day I'd stand by the door, ready to greet him, making what I thought were valiant efforts to calm him down and control his arrival. This whirlwind behavior continued throughout the day. I made sure to stay near Ben to support him at the beginning of each activity and transition. I guess the rest of the class figured out that Ben needed me and just sort of tolerated my giving him most of my attention. By the end of each day, I was totally exhausted. I tried to talk with his mother about getting him evaluated, but she wouldn't hear of it.

Pamela explained that she documented many observations to share with his mother in the hope that they would be useful if he were tested. Here are a few of her notes.

10/14, 9:00 a.m.

Group time—B raises hand, waves wildly. I call on him. He stutters, " Em, em, I, I." Shakes his head, purses lips, stops speaking. (written after group time: This is typical of meeting behavior.)

10/25, 8:25 a.m.

Arrival time—B runs into room; calls, "Hello." Starts for coat hooks, turns quickly toward cubbies, stops short, bumps into Simon. S: " Watch out, Ben!" B: "Sorry." B shakes head, stands still for moment. Looks around. Rushes toward coat hooks. Drops backpack. Rushes to art table with coat still on. Leans over to see Rachel's drawing. Takes coat off; sleeve swipes table, knocks Rachel's crayons to floor. R: " Ben, careful." Ben goes to rug, sits down with coat still partially on.

Very often, at the end of the day when Pamela saw Ronny, her principal, in the hall or the teacher's room, she needed to recount her recent experiences with Ben. After several weeks, Ronny shared her observations of Pamela with her. She explained that Pamela appeared stressed, overly focused on Ben, and missing many of the positive things that were going on in her classroom. Ronny suggested to Pamela that her constant vigilance of Ben was not necessarily helping him and that the other children also needed her attention. Moreover, she urged Pamela to observe the other children as a way to regain some of her own enthusiasm about teaching. To encourage her, Ronny gave Pamela an assignment: Pamela was not to observe Ben formally for one week. Instead she was to tell Ronny about someone else in the class every day.

Reflection

Pamela was amazed at the result of Ronny's suggestions.

> At first it was a struggle for me to shift my attention away from Ben. It had become a habit for me to observe his behavior. I worked at reporting each day to Ronny about *another* child or an activity that had taken place. Ben's behavior improved as I gave him more opportunities to work independently. Other children stepped in to support Ben when necessary.

Just as Ronny had predicted, Pamela was less tired, and her enthusiasm for her class and their work was renewed.

Next steps

By the end of the week, Pamela had gained a different perspective about Ben. She began to realize that she had been trying to manage Ben's behavior instead of encouraging him to regulate it himself. By doing so, she had lost sight of the needs of the rest of the group. Ben's mother continued to decline additional evaluation and intervention, but Ben was making some gains in the classroom. Pamela's energy increased, and the overall dynamics of the classroom improved.

Using What You Learn for Assessment and Reporting

In this book, we have emphasized the power of observation in building relationships and responding to children in ways that foster their competence. Observation and documentation are the bases for assessing children's learning. Assessment is the process of asking questions about children's learning and development and then collecting evidence that helps you answer those questions in order to make good decisions about teaching.

You observe in an ongoing way, asking questions and making new discoveries about children and your program. Periodically, you reach a checkpoint or a time to evaluate the information you collected by observing. That is when you review the data you have accumulated and make some judgments. You ask yourself, "What does this information tell me? "How is this child progressing?" "How is this child performing?" You compare the documentation you have collected with learning goals, outcomes, and standards.

Patterns emerge as you study your observation notes. For example, you may identify children who would benefit from more practice of or direct instruction about a certain skill. You may realize such things as the fact that, while you have been focusing on the goal of promoting children's communication skills, you were not paying enough attention to promoting gross motor development.

In many programs, teachers use formal instruments to structure the assessment process. Some programs develop their own systems. Whatever assessment and reporting system you use, it is essential for it to be compatible with your program's goals and objectives and for you to use it on an ongoing basis.

Sorting and Organizing Data

Caroline has gathered extensive observation notes and work samples. In mid-November, she reviews them in order to complete the assessment forms her preschool program uses. She organizes her notes at least once each week so that she can review them efficiently. She explains,

> The biggest discovery I made about observation and assessment was that, when my observation notes included details, I could relate them more easily to many of the goals and objectives that I try to address in my program. When I first started observing, I wrote just a word or two. I rarely included quotes of what the children said. Now I focus on three or four children each day so that I observe every child at least once every week. On Friday, I spend about 15 minutes during rest time to look over my observation notes and work samples for the week, writing the numbers of the relevant objectives right on the notes and samples. As I got better at taking notes, I found that most observations relate to at least three or four objectives. Here's an example:

4/24, Jacquie

Writing center—J announces that she made birthday card for her sister. Used markers, stickers, red paper. J asks T: "Want me to read it to you?" T: "Yes." As she reads, J points to each word: HAPY BRDY SHALIA. YOU R MI FVRT STR.

> This observation took about 2 minutes, and I was able to interact with Jacquie while I conducted it. It gave me information about many skills on the checklist I use, including writing, print awareness, speaking, and the purposeful use of materials.

Discovering Gaps in What You Know

As teachers review their documentation for assessment, they often find that they need even more information. As you will see in the stories that follow, the information gaps that teachers discover sometimes relate to children and sometimes to curriculum.

> Kyla was in my second-grade class last year. After the first 8 weeks of the year, I sat down to organize and review my assessment information and to prepare for family conferences. I didn't have much to say about Kyla. She seemed to be the perfect second grader. Yes, I know that I'm not supposed to be judgmental, but she completed assignments easily and independently and was willing to help when asked by adults and children. I looked through my observation notes, only to discover that none of my anecdotes related to her specifically. The samples in her portfolio showed careful and detailed work, but I wasn't sure what interested her or what her talents are. I wasn't ready to talk with Kyla's parents in a way that would convey that I know their child.
>
> I made some decisions and jotted down questions to ask her parents: What does Kyla like to do at home? What makes her laugh? What does she say about school? What are their goals for Kyla? I decided to observe Kyla each day for a week and noted in my plan book different times of the day I would observe. By the time the conference came, I had useful information to share about Kyla: She liked to write stories but wasn't ready to share them in class, and she loved her new kitten, Gypsy. At the conference, her parents told me that she was very nervous about school and afraid to try new things. After that, things changed. I encouraged Kyla's writing, and, by midyear, she worked with a few others to create our class newspaper.

◆　　◆　　◆　　◆　　◆　　◆

I had never seen 5-year-old Darren write. At journal time, he either chatted with others at his table or drew in his journal with a pencil. He responded with details when I asked him to tell me about his picture, but he didn't want to add written words. He also did not want me to write the ideas he talked about.

One day when he was in the dramatic play area that had been set up as a pizza shop, Darren was pretending to be the waiter. The props included an order pad and a pencil. Darren was busy taking orders on the pad. I joined the children's play and was surprised to see that he had written *PIZZA* and the names of the children. Now I can document his emerging writing skills. I realized that I was focusing all of my attention on whether he was writing during journal time. I needed to look for opportunities to encourage his writing skills during choice time.

As they review their documentation to complete assessments, teachers sometimes find that they do not have enough evidence to assess children on particular developmental objectives. When you do not have enough information, you have to gather more data about what each child knows and can do. For example, Phyllis's teacher realized that she did not have information about the phonological awareness of most of her preschool children. Here's what she shared.

I've been teaching preschool for many years. I have always recited and sung fingerplays, songs, and rhymes with my children. However, it is only recently, and as a result of attending workshops, that I understand what *phonological awareness* means and how these activities help children acquire this awareness. I usually conduct phonological awareness activities with the whole group, so it is challenging for me to document individual children's learning.

I realized I didn't have enough information about the children's phonological awareness and that I had to make an effort to focus on individual children at various times of the day. I also realized that I had to incorporate rhyming and other language games into my informal interactions with children. After I changed what I was doing, I had many more anecdotes about individual children's phonological awareness skills.

More importantly, I now understand how to use what I'm learning in workshops to extend children's learning. When I heard Brooke say, "I love this yummy apple," at snack time, I responded, "This snack is yummy. Can you make it disappear into your tummy? I wonder, Brooke, do you know how to cook?" We then went around the table and rhymed each child's name.

Identifying Questions and the Need for Further Evaluation

Have you ever worked with a child whom you just didn't understand? No matter how you modified instruction, varied your schedule and routines, or changed activities, you weren't sure how the child experienced them. In these situations, purposeful observation and thoughtful interpretation of the data you collect can help you clarify the type of information you still need. That leads to more questions and sometimes the need to seek the assistance of other professionals. Consider David's experience with Reggie.

David has been a kindergarten teacher in a suburban public school system for more than 15 years. He is relatively new to systematic observation. "Since I began observing systematically," he explains, "I spend more time watching how children do things. I tend to focus on two or three children a week."

Lately, David has found Reggie's behavior challenging. David describes him as "hard to engage, always moving around, and often off-task." David decided to focus his observations of Reggie. Over the past 2 months, he recorded the following observations:

Readers'/writers' workshop—R spent 15 minutes drawing hungry caterpillar. Moved around in chair, tapped pencil on table, and squinted when I encouraged him to try writing the words of his story.

3/19, 11:00

Large-group—While reading recipe chart, R tilted head and appeared to look out of corners of eyes. Squinted while looking at chart. Looked at pictures but did not seem to know what they represented.

4/14, 10:30

Small-group—Walk along nature trail—Children called out when they found something interesting. R repeatedly asked, "Where is it?" Sometimes R was on other side of trail; insects were gone by time he joined other children. When R was with group, he looked all around area but not at what other children were examining. Had difficulty walking on path; kept tripping.

4/28, 2:30

One-on-one—Asked R to write his name on class thank-you note to grocery store. R tilted head; squinted at card; asked, "What are those marks on it?" I read the message aloud and again asked him to write name on card. He picked up marker, tapped it, made dots and lines on card.

4/30, 11:00

One-on-one (reevaluation of ability to write own name)—Provided 6" x 6" card with R's name written in large letters. R looked at card; said, "That's my name." I asked him to write his name on thank-you note. R picked up marker, looked at his name card, wrote each letter of his name on note. Looked at me and smiled.

Reflection

David saw a pattern in Reggie's behavior and accomplishments over the last 4 months when he reviewed his notes and filled out an "Individual Child Profile." He explains,

> I had wondered briefly if Reggie had trouble seeing, but I was involved in trying to help him pay attention to what he was doing. When I reviewed my notes, I realized that I had good reasons to suspect a visual problem. I wondered whether a vision problem is the reason for his distractibility or whether there is another reason. While continuing my observations, I spoke to the resource teacher, who had observed many of the same behaviors.

Next steps

David shared this information with the school nurse, who contacted Reggie's mother about having his vision evaluated. She took him to an eye doctor, who discovered a severe problem in Reggie's left eye. He now wears a patch on his right eye and will get glasses soon.

David explains, "I am figuring out how to support Reggie." One of David's strategies is to ask Reggie to describe what he sees before he attempts a task. For example, yesterday his description alerted David to that fact that Reggie could not see the numbers on the left side of a game board. David and the children Reggie was playing with read the numbers to him and wrote them on large cards so he could play. David made an appointment to talk with the nurse about her ideas and suggestions, and he plans to meet with Reggie's parents. "I want to be sure that Reggie is physically safe as he adjusts to the patch and that he has positive learning experiences at school."

Although David has questions about Reggie's distractibility, he has decided to focus now on helping Reggie compensate for his limited vision. When Reggie gets his glasses, David plans to continue observing and thinking about Reggie's sometimes limited concentration.

Working Together With Families

Children benefit when the important adults in their lives work together to get to know them and to understand and meet their needs. Teachers can share their observations with families in many different ways. Families also can contribute what they notice at home. Sharing observations validates the sometimes different perspectives of families and teachers and makes communication an open, ongoing process.

In this section, we see how a teacher and family observe together before deciding how to respond to a child. We also see how joint observation can strengthen partnerships that support a child's development.

Deciding With Families How to Respond

Sara, an infant–toddler teacher, shares this story:

> Ellen is 22 months old. Her parents talked with me, upset because they think she is selfish. "She is always grabbing things," they told me. I suggested that we observe her together to answer their question, "Why does Ellen grab?" Then together we can plan ways to support Ellen. They agreed, and her mother arranged to stay for a few hours one morning. While we watched Ellen, I jotted this note:

6/3, 11:00 a.m.

Ellen picks up toy cell phone. Presses numbers, holds it to her ear. Talks. Puts the phone down on the table. Reaches for a dress-up hat; puts it on. Turns back to the table. Another child has picked up the phone Ellen had been using. Ellen yells, "No!" and reaches for the phone.

I intervened by getting a second toy phone from the shelf and giving it to Ellen, saying. "Here is another phone for you to use." Ellen's mother and I talked about what we saw and heard. We reviewed my notes and agreed on the facts about what we had observed. Then I suggested, "Let's think about what happened from Ellen's perspective."

After talking about what we had observed and how Ellen might have perceived the situation, we decided that Ellen wasn't necessarily being selfish. It appeared as though she hadn't finished playing with the phone. Perhaps she had a plan in mind: Maybe she wanted to keep talking on the phone after she put on a hat. Someone had taken her phone, so she could not continue her pretend conversation.

We talked about how long it takes children to learn how to share and that having duplicate toys and materials is a good strategy to use when helping children learn to get along with each other.

Ellen's mom said, "There's a lot more to understanding children than I thought. I think I see why you brought over another phone. If it had been up to me, I would have taken the phone from Ellen and told her she had to share."

Later that day, I saw Ellen hold out the rubber giraffe to another child. I told her parents about this. Together we decided to keep observing Ellen at the program and that her parents would record some of their observations at home, too. Then we set an appointment to meet in 2 weeks to talk about what Ellen is experiencing and to decide how we could support her.

Strengthening Family Ties

Leslie, a second-grade teacher in a rural school, shares observations about how to strengthen the ties between a grandmother and granddaughter. She explains,

> Last year, Catherine needed a great deal of guidance in order to manage her behavior, which tended to be violent and aggressive. Her grandmother often came in to help her, too. When I scheduled my home visit this year, I decided to try a different approach. I told her grandmother that I wouldn't call her only when there was a problem; I would also let her know about the positive things Catherine was doing in school. We decided that I would send home a daily note.

Leslie began sharing simple observations, beginning with notes about mostly positive behaviors. They showed her appreciation of Catherine and her desire to be objective about how to support Catherine's development. The notes also helped Leslie and Catherine's grandmother begin building a partnership. Leslie had to think carefully about Catherine's strengths. Here are a few examples of her observations and how she shared them in the notes she sent to Catherine's grandmother.

9/6

During group discussion about favorite foods, Catherine pulled on her shoelace while listening to another child. Waited for turn to speak; said that her favorite food is blueberry pancakes and that she could eat 100 of them. C smiled when three other children agreed.

Note home: Today Catherine waited for her turn to speak during a group discussion. She told the class how much she loves blueberry pancakes, declaring that they are her favorite food and that she could eat 100 of them!

10/1

Catherine spent 15 minutes drawing and writing in her
writer's journal about a dog named Henry who likes to
roll in the mud and chase cats.

Note home: Today Catherine spent 15 minutes drawing
and writing a story about a dog named Henry!

10/13

Catherine's face tightened when Paul crumpled the
edge of her painting. C moved her hands toward him as
if to pinch him. C looked at me and called for help.
I brought both children together; we talked about
what had happened. P explained that he crumpled C's
painting by accident when he tried to hang his painting
on drying line. P told C that he was sorry. C looked
at P and listened to what he was saying. She smiled;
said, "That's okay. Do you want me to help you hang
the painting, Paul?" Together they hung their paintings
on line. I told her she helped to solve classroom
problem.

Note home: Today Catherine helped solve a conflict
with another child by asking for a teacher's help. The
children helped each other hang their paintings.

Reflection

Leslie has used her observations to build a positive relationship with Catherine and to strengthen Catherine's relationship with her grandmother. Her grandmother is an ally in supporting Catherine at home and in school. Leslie explained,

> Sharing my observations has had a significant impact on Catherine, on her grandmother, and on me. Catherine's confidence seems to be growing. She smiled when she told me that her grandmother is proud of her. When I asked her how she knows that, she said, "She hugs me a lot and hangs up the notes you send." Catherine's grandmother has called me to say how much she appreciates the positive notes. I think she is seeing Catherine in a more positive light and, hopefully, beginning to see school as her partner in helping Catherine develop and learn.

> I have built a good relationship with Catherine and her grandmother. I asked Catherine why she thought she needed help in calming down so many times last year. She told me she wasn't able to tell her side of the story when there was a problem and that made her angry. I asked what she could do without hurting others when she gets angry. She said, "I could get you or ask them why they did something." I told Catherine that those were two ideas that would help solve problems. Catherine and her grandmother talk every day about the notes that I send home. They discuss what Catherine did each day and sometimes what she might have done differently. Together they are making a scrapbook of Catherine's successes in school.

Next steps

Leslie plans to continue observing Catherine and communicating with Catherine's grandmother. She usually sends home notes about positive behaviors. She wants to build on their growing mutual trust by beginning to share some of Catherine's behavioral challenges. She plans to offer Catherine's grandmother ideas about what she can do at home to help Catherine learn to manage frustration and anger in socially acceptable ways.

Sharing Observations Over Time to Support a Child

Sharon, a family child care provider, describes her experiences sharing observations with two families. She explains,

> Building good working relationships with families takes time and patience. Some partnerships are easier to build than others.
>
> Take the Jillsons for example. Kendra was an alert, smiley, curious baby who was thriving in many ways. However, her clothes were often torn and dirty and, when I changed her diaper, I often found she hadn't been cleaned well. On some cold days she arrived without a jacket, and once she came without socks. Twice I needed to send her home because she was so sick when she arrived.
>
> I observed and shared with her parents my notes about Kendra's progress, about her delight in the world, and about her physical care. In terms of her physical care, nothing changed for the 2 years Kendra was in my program. I often felt angry and frustrated with her parents because of that. Finding a colleague to talk with about my feelings helped me remember that the most important thing was to support Kendra. I cleaned her when she was dirty and dressed her in a donated jacket when she came without one on cold days.
>
> Working with Rebecca Reilly was a rewarding experience. I was concerned that her 2-year-old, Jerry, was not talking clearly. He was new to my program.

Sharon began observing Jerry in December. At the same time, she took steps to get to know his mother and to establish mutual trust. For example, she always greeted Rebecca warmly, asked how things were going, and regularly shared information about Jerry's day. At the end of January, she arranged a conference with Jerry's mother. Here are a few of the observation notes she shares.

12/5

During neighborhood walk, Jerry tugs on my sweater and talks excitedly, raising and lowering voice. He gestures across the street. I see big dog tied to parking meter.

12/18

Jerry joins Sam and Valerie, who are constructing road with cardboard blocks and placing rubber farm animals along it. J speaks. S looks at him and at V; asks, "What did he say?" V looks at J and then S. They go back to building without responding to J. J stands in block area, looking at them and frowning. J kicks at blocks. I step in.

1/6

We are making playdough. Jerry carefully pours cup of water into flour mixture. He picks up wooden spoon; stirs; says, "I do it." Smiles at me.

1/11

I walked over to Jerry and Trina; asked them to begin putting their puzzles away. J looked up, smiled, continued working on puzzle. T began to put her puzzle away. J looked at her and then picked up his puzzle and carried it to shelf.

Reflection

Sharon talks about the most effective way to share her concerns with Jerry's mother, Rebecca:

I considered whether Jerry might have trouble hearing and thought about how to discuss that possibility with his mother. I knew it was a difficult time for her. She is a single mother and was just beginning a new job.

I decided to share with her many of my observations of Jerry's strengths and skills. Then I raised my concern about his hearing and language development. I began by explaining to Rebecca that I want Jerry to get the full benefit of being in child care. Then I said that I wanted to talk with her about some of my other observations. I shared observations of times when both the children and I had trouble understanding Jerry's speech and observations of his reactions in some of these situations. As Rebecca listened, her back stiffened, and I could see tears forming in her eyes. "I have to go," she told me, and she left.

Jerry's neighbor brought him and picked him up for the next 3 days. On the third day, I called and spoke with Rebecca, asking her to come in early the next morning so that she can tell me about how Jerry interacts with others at home and about how she supports him. I suggested that we develop an action plan together to support Jerry's development and to help him get all of the benefits of the program. She came in with him the following morning. When we greeted each other, Rebecca said, "I appreciate your phone call and commitment to Jerry's development. What can we do?"

Next steps

Sharon and Rebecca discussed what they had observed at school and at home and decided to continue sharing their observations of Jerry during the next month. They set up times to talk on the phone in the evening when Jerry was in bed. They agreed that, if they still had concerns at the end of the month, Sharon would find out where Rebecca could take Jerry for hearing and language evaluations and that Rebecca would take him. Although Sharon wanted Jerry to be tested right away, she realized that the month would give both Rebecca and her time to collect more information. Communicating with each other would also strengthen their partnership, which would benefit Jerry. Sharon and Rebecca also exchanged a few simple strategies that they had found successful in supporting Jerry's attempts to communicate.

SUMMING UP

The teachers in these stories have a variety of questions to answer. Their reasons for observing ranged from figuring out why a toddler was biting to discovering how to encourage a preschooler to express her ideas in both her home language and English. One teacher tried to understand the seemingly disruptive behavior of a second grader and its possible effect on the group. By observing, they gained insights about children's strengths, knowledge, interests, and skills. Then they used what they learned by observing to

- **Support individual children.** Children, like all of us, learn best when they have trusting relationships with their teachers and when learning experiences are meaningful. Observation gives you the information you need to build better relationships with children and shape instruction according to the strengths and needs of each child.

- **Respond to individuals and to the group.** This includes intervening to support individual children, extending children's learning, responding to the group, and balancing group and individual needs.

- **Respond to the group.** Responding to the group requires a great deal of thoughtful planning. At the same time, it requires a willingness to modify your plans according to the group's mood and dynamics, interests, knowledge, and skills.

- **Conduct assessments and report.** As you interpret the information you have about each child, you make judgments about the child's development and learning. Patterns emerge that help you make decisions about future interactions with children and plan the strategies and activities you will use to promote their learning.

- **Work together with families.** Children benefit when they see adults working together. Observing and exchanging information with families helps you learn more about their children, and working together with family members helps all of you continue to support children's development and learning as their strengths and needs change.

We have talked extensively about how observation gives you the information you need to respond to children in a variety of situations. In the final chapter, we turn our attention to how to start observing and how to make it a habit.

Getting Started: Observing Every Day

For most of us, learning something new requires lots of practice. Recall when you first learned to drive, made a new recipe, or used a particular software program for the first time. Each step was labored, you were aware of every action. But after awhile, and with practice, it became second nature. This is true of observing as well.

But how do you get started? And once you begin, how do you keep on going? This chapter begins with some tips for getting started with observing, some reasons to keep on going, and strategies to make observation part of your daily routine. In addition, we answer frequently asked questions about observing.

Tips for Getting Started

The caregivers and teachers we talked with confirm that once you begin observing regularly, you get hooked. However, getting started demands conscious effort. We recommend that you set up a structure that forces you to observe and record regularly and then to reflect on what you've observed.

We asked many teachers for advice on how to get started as a more purposeful observer. Here are some of their tips.

Remember, There's No Time Like the Present

Most of us are good at coming up with excuses to keep us from tackling something new. "I can't start until I have all the class routines in order." "I'll start next month, when I have a little more time." "I'll start when my new assistant arrives." When it comes to observing, you can begin anytime. As one third-grade teacher said:

> Whenever you begin, you're sure to learn something interesting.

Don't Let Worries About Doing It Right Get in Your Way

Many teachers feel that they aren't going about observing in the right way, so they end up not observing at all. In the words of one teacher:

> I'm the type of person who wants to do it right. Since I'm not really sure what I'm supposed to do and how I'm supposed to organize my notes, I'm too nervous. I can't seem to get started.

Observing is an ongoing learning process and, no matter how many years you spend observing children, you will refine your methods continually.

Find Something Interesting to Watch and Watch It

Some teachers find that the best way to begin is just to look around. When something interesting happens, stop what you are doing, take 2 minutes, and look and listen. Make a few notes about what you see and hear. Try this once a day for a week and see how much you learn. Or select one skill or set of related skills that you don't know very much about. Make a matrix for your class, then begin observing. You might be surprised by how much more you know than you thought you did.

Work With a Colleague

Working with a partner often makes a new task more enjoyable and easier to handle. Your observing partner can be someone who works in your room, next door, or down the hall. Take turns observing. If you don't share a classroom, combine your children in one room for a story or other activity. One of you leads and the other observes a few children. Alternatively, go to your partner's room when your children are at music or art. Then switch. Talk with each other about what you saw. A second-grade teacher shares her enthusiasm:

> You can't really learn to be a good observer alone. Partner up. Go to another teacher's room. Observe for her. Talk about what you saw. Let your partner come to your room and observe. You'll be so amazed at what each of you saw, how different your perceptions were. It is great to have someone to bounce ideas off of—someone to say, "Hey, I never thought about it like that."

Start Small

Give yourself a manageable assignment. Decide who and what you want to observe and set a time limit. For example:

- Observe children in terms of a particular skill or set of skills for one week. You might want to watch and listen to how children use language, interact with peers, or use strategies to solve problems. Generate a few questions related to the skill to help you know what to watch for. If you are observing language use, for example, you might ask yourself:

    - Do the children use single words or speak in sentences?

    - Are they asking questions and, if so, what kinds?

    - Do they use language to express feelings?

    - What kind of language do they use to retell a story?

- Observe two or three children for a week. Like this infant caregiver, you might select children you don't know very well.

  I focus on observing two babies each week. It doesn't mean I don't pay attention to the others, but having "focus children" helps ensure that I don't get so caught up in daily routines that I forget to observe.

- Have a conversation with a different child each day and jot down some notes either during the conversation or right after. A second-grade teacher said:

  I have intentional conversations with children to gain insight about how they think. Before I was a regular observer, I didn't stop and listen carefully to what children were saying.

- Observe at the same time each day for one week. For example, if you work with babies, you might want to observe during arrival each day for a week. With older children you might decide to observe during snack, choice time, or when the children write in their journals. You might want to concentrate on a few children for the week, a different child each day, or whoever catches your interest at the time.

Acknowledge and Appreciate How Much You Can Learn From Observation

When you finish an observation, or at the end of week, review your notes. Ask yourself, "What did I learn?" Chances are there will be some surprises. As a toddler teacher discovered:

Observing is a bit like exercise. Everyone knows they should do it. The challenge is getting to the gym and starting. With exercise, once you see yourself gaining strength or losing weight, you're hooked!

Take a Moment to Think About What You Have Learned

When you finish an observation, or at the end of the week, review your notes. Ask yourself, "What did I learn, and how can I apply it?" As a teacher of toddlers discovered:

> You'll learn about kids and yourself in leaps and bounds. With observing, you uncover a gold mine of information. The thought and time you devote to observing is much smaller than the rewards you will reap.

Reflect on the Rewards of Observation

In talking with teachers, we discovered that in addition to providing helpful information about children, the act of observing affects the culture of the program. Here are stories about how spending time tuning in to individual children changed the climate of the program and teachers' perceptions of their roles.

A teacher of toddlers shared:

> As our staff has become better observers, our program has changed. We support one another more, so each of us has more one-on-one time observing and interacting with the children. One-on-one time is really the way to go—I know I feel better about myself when I'm doing more responsive caregiving.

Teachers of older children described how the children became more accepting of their one-on-one time with others, once they understood what the teacher was doing when she was observing and that they, too, would get a turn for undivided attention. A first-grade teacher noted:

> I think the culture in my room is very different now. For one, kids know from experience that I take the time to talk with them and really listen. They look forward to their conversations with me—if they don't get to show me their work today, they know they'll get a chance tomorrow.

A veteran second-grade teacher talked about how she came to see her role differently. As she stepped back, the children relied more on each other and used each other as resources:

> I've been teaching for 20 years. Until recently I was pretty traditional—lots of whole group instruction. As I've gotten more into observing, I structure many more small group activities. This gives me much more one-on-one time with children. They rely more on each other now than they used to.

Teachers shared stories about how their actions as observers increased children's motivation and pride in their work. This teacher discovered that her recording strategy, devised to help her remember to observe, had the added benefit of increasing children's competence:

> I keep a sheet of paper for each child on the front wall under the chalkboard. When I see a child do or say something I want to remember, I jot it down on a sticky and put it on that child's sheet. I started this system to make sure I was observing everyone. It has turned into a means of showing children my respect. They frequently ask me to write things down and call me to come and see specific things they are doing. They take great pride in the fact that I notice and care enough to write notes about them.

A preschool teacher told a story about how interested her children were in what she was writing:

> At first I felt that I shouldn't let the children know what I was doing. I kept trying to observe and record by sneaking around. Then one day a child said, "Hey, what are you writing?" I told him that I was writing down things I observed. With a big grin he said, "Write something down about me." I guess I was slow to see the advantages of letting the children know. For one, the children get so excited about showing me what they are doing. When they see the teacher write down what they are doing—it must be significant—it gives more importance to their work. I also think that my writing observations models literacy for them.

A kindergarten teacher told us how observing made him appreciate how much children know. For him, learning to listen to children resulted in children becoming more independent and confident:

> I really learn interesting things about kids by listening to them, especially when I eavesdrop on the conversations they have with each other. I'm constantly amazed by how much children learn from one another—in fact, how much they actually know about things I didn't know they know. This is a new realization for me, something I didn't really value before. I think they've picked up on it. As I spend more time showing respect for children's knowledge by stepping back and listening, they spend more time exchanging information and ideas with one another.

We encourage you to take some time for reflection. As you begin observing, or continue to observe, think about how what you are doing affects you, the children, and your program.

A second-grade teacher sums it up:

> Once you see its value, it is hard to stop observing.

Make Observation Part Of Your Daily Routine

Over time, observing and recording will become more natural, and the formal structures you've used to get started will lessen in importance. As a first-grade teacher said:

> Once you get into a routine and rhythm, you've got it.

The caregivers and teachers we have talked with confirm that, once you begin observing, you get hooked. But to make observing a habit, you have to make it fit your daily routine. As one infant caregiver put it:

> I want to get to where observing is like a healthy lifestyle, not a diet I struggle to follow.

To incorporate observing into your schedule, set aside time for observing, recording, and reflecting just as you plan for the other activities and routines of the day and week. Here are some ideas caregivers and teachers have shared.

- Identify one or two times during the day or week when you can easily step out of the action and watch what children are doing. Write the word "OBSERVATION" right into your schedule so that you remember to do it. Here's what one toddler caregiver said about this:

  I have to set up observation like any daily routine. I put it in my schedule: Wednesdays 10:00–10:15 Observing. When you spend 8 hours a day for 5 days each week with children, you can find 10 minutes to observe.

- If you work with preschool- or school-age children, plan some time each day when they can work or play independently or in small groups. This will allow you to step out of the action and observe for a few minutes.

- Select an activity each day during which you know you can observe and record in the midst of the action. Some teachers decide in advance who they will observe, while others wait to see who catches their eye.

- Review a checklist biweekly or monthly to see what you already know and what you need to learn about individual children. Review your schedule for the week to determine when you might be able to find the information you are looking for. Note the times and what you want to focus on in your weekly plans. For example, in reviewing her checklist, a third-grade teacher notices that she needs information about Joanna's scientific thinking skills. She sees that a science activity is planned for Thursday morning and notes in her plans to observe Joanna during that time.

- Take time to reflect on what you have observed. You may want to take a few minutes to jot notes at the end of each day.

Closing Thoughts

It's very easy to get caught up in the "how-tos" of observation and lose sight of its power to make a difference in your work with children. "Should I record my observations on index cards or large stickies?" "Should I observe only during choice time?" "Should I record running records or use a rating scale?"

It isn't that the specifics don't matter—they do—but only as a means to the end—a means to getting to know, respect, and appreciate children and to intervene in ways that enable them to be successful learners. Otherwise we just end up with a stack of notes crumpled up in the back of a drawer.

As we've discussed in this book, observing is an attitude of openness, necessary for good teaching. We hope we have convinced you to become aware of yourself as an observer and to take full advantage of the rich insights observing offers you every day. Watching, listening, reflecting, and relating are as important as anything else you do during the day. The children and their families will benefit. And so will you.

Observing can make teaching more personally and intellectually satisfying. There's nothing more rewarding than coming to understand and appreciate a child whom you didn't really like or found puzzling. Without observing, Amy would have continued to see Johnny as chaotic, Margo's picture of Tony would have been limited by what others had said, and Judy would have not been able to get past her feelings to discover Rachel's enthusiasm and sense of humor.

It is energizing to learn and to succeed in making a connection with a child or family that seemed outside your reach. As an engaged learner, you will imbue your setting with a sense of the importance and rewards of being open to learning. Your curiosity, questioning, and reflecting will lead you to new insights and to modeling learning and growing for the children and families in your group. Yours will truly be an environment where the young—and not so young—are encouraged to explore and discover.

As we have said before, the key to your success as an observer is making observation work for you. While there are guidelines to follow, the decisions you make every day as you begin to observe regularly must take into account your preferences and needs. It won't always be easy. You are sure to come up against obstacles sooner or later. But we guarantee, if you make a commitment to observe children regularly, your teaching will become more interesting, rewarding, and effective.

Appendices

The Power of Learning With Others: A Study Guide

Since we wrote the first edition of *The Power of Observation* in 1999, many people have told us that they have taken ideas from our book to promote professional development in child care centers, family child care networks, schools, and college classrooms. We have often been asked to create a study guide that offers additional ideas. It is our pleasure to include a guide in this new edition.

The study guide is organized in the same way as the rest of the book. There is one section for each chapter. Each section includes:

- A brief overview of the main points covered in the chapter

- Three to five discussion questions to help you apply the content of the chapter to everyday practice

- Two to four exercises that can be used during staff meetings and classes and as the basis of professional development assignments

Please adapt and use these ideas to make them helpful for your program. Pick and choose those you find most useful for the people with whom you work.

Setting the Stage

We begin by discussing strategies that set the stage for teaching and learning about observation.

The Power of Observation focuses on the importance of building relationships with children in order to foster their competence and success. We believe strongly that relationships are at the core of learning for everyone, children and adults alike. You set the stage for teaching and learning about observation when you build positive relationships with your colleagues and create a collaborative adult learning community focusing on observation. Here is a list of strategies to get you started:

Visit classrooms regularly, formally and informally, to get to know each teacher's classroom and teaching style. Frequent visits will allow teachers to relax when you are in their classrooms and teach as they do when you are not there.

Remember that one of the most effective ways to teach about observation is by modeling the practice. When you observe,

- Watch and listen to children and teachers objectively.

- Look for specific teacher behaviors related to observing and individualizing.

- Make validating comments to children and teachers about what you see and hear.

Engage in reflective conversations about what you see and hear. Use open-ended questions. Remember, you are modeling language that you want students and staff members to use in their everyday work with children and families.

Here are some prompts to start conversations:

- I saw... Tell me more about ...

- What do you think…might be experiencing?

- Have you talked this over with ...?

- What do you think might explain ...?

- Have you tried ...?

- What else could you try...?

Discuss children and their work in the following ways:

- Study samples of children's work and explain what the children were learning.

- Watch a video clip together and discuss the following: What do we see? What might it mean? What might I do?

- Bring documentation of one child's development and learning (observation notes and portfolio samples) and discuss what the child knows, what the child is ready to learn, and strategies for supporting the child.

- Role-play the use of observation and documentation in family-teacher conferences.

Chapter 1: Introduction

The first chapter explains the basic premises of the book:

- Observation is watching and listening to learn.

- Observation gives you the information you need to build positive relationships with individual children.

- Getting to know children gives you the information you need to be an effective decision maker.

- Observing well requires an attitude of openness. Observation involves wondering and learning about children.

- Wondering and asking, observing and documenting, and reflecting and responding are central to your role as a teacher.

Discussion Questions

- How did you react to the authors' personal stories about observing and teaching? In what ways did their perceptions about the children change because of new information they gained by observing?

- Refer to the reflection questions on page 8.

  - How do you view the relationship between observing and teaching?

  - Is observation something you struggle to find time to do? Is it an extra task on your to-do list?

  - Is observation part of your everyday teaching? Was it always that way, or did something cause a shift?

- Would you like to share a personal story about how your perception of a child changed because of your observations?

Exercises

1. **What is the connection between observing and teaching?**

    Working with a learning partner, list the top five responsibilities of a teacher.

    Discuss how each responsibility is supported by observation.

    Share your list and insights with the group.

2. **Explain the connection between observing and teaching.**

    Imagine that you were explaining the important connection between observing and teaching to a parent or new teacher. Explain this connection as you role-play.

Chapter 2: Using Observation to Build Relationships

This chapter addresses four key ideas about how observation helps teachers build positive relationships with children. It helps them

- Get to know each child

- Show respect for and appreciation of each child

- Make a connection with each child

- Foster each child's competence and success

Discussion Questions

- Think of someone with whom you have a very positive relationship, who accepts you and appreciates your accomplishments. How do you feel when you are with that person? What does that person say and do that makes you feel that way?

- How do you show children respect and appreciation?

- What are some examples of nonjudgmental comments you can make when talking with children about their work?

- Do you have a child whom you find difficult to understand? Review pages 21–22. How can observation help you get to know this child?

Exercises

1. **What do you know about the children you teach?**

   Fold a sheet of paper in thirds, holding it the long way.

   In the first column, list the names of all of the children in your program. Write their names in 90 seconds or less.

   Were you able to list everyone? Did you forget anyone?

   In the middle column, write something you've learned about each child.

   Share and discuss your lists with a partner. Using the categories of things to learn about a child on pages 14–15, label what you know about each child.

   In the third column, write an "I wonder" statement about each child.

   With the whole group, share ideas of what you might do to discover what you want to learn about each child.

   Close this activity by discussing this question: How can you use what you know about each child to build a relationship with that child?

2. **How can you get to know an "invisible child"?**

   Who is the child whom you didn't think of at first?

   Why do you think this was so?

   Working in pairs, brainstorm strategies to get to know this child.

   Share your ideas with the whole group.

3. **Think about the power of having a teacher who knows you well.**

   How does it feel to be with someone who knows you very, very well?

   How does this relate to our work with young children? Why is it so important to build positive relationships with all children?

4. **What are the challenges of getting to know individual children in a group setting?**

   Brainstorm reasons why it is sometimes difficult to get to know individual children in a group setting.

   What strategies can help you overcome these barriers?

Chapter 3 : You as Observer

Chapter 3 discusses the personal side of observation and strategies teachers can use to ensure that their documentation of children's development and learning is objective.

- Be aware of what you bring to observation: your culture, temperament, interests, feelings, and professional expertise.

- Strive to write observation notes that record facts about children's behavior rather than interpretations of or judgments about their behavior.

Discussion Questions

- What factors influence what you see and hear when you observe?

- Describe a time when you misunderstood or misjudged an individual or situation. How can being aware that this can happen to you help you become a more effective observer?

- What can you do to maintain your awareness of what you bring to observation and how those factors affect your interpretations?

Exercises

1. **What do individuals bring to observation?**

   Without looking around, write a description of the room we are in.

   Compare observations: Did some people notice more than others? Did some people describe an object in great detail? Did some give the big picture? Did some focus on a particular aspect of the room, such as the colors, furnishings, or people?

   What does this say about the power of what you bring to observation?

2. **What do you bring to observation?**

   As you observe this week, be aware of your filters, the factors that affect what and how you see.

   Jot down the factors.

   Bring your list to share with the group.

3. **What is the difference between factual information and the interpretation of facts?**

   List five things you know about a child.

   Look over your list with a learning partner.

   Discuss and then label each point as "fact" or "judgment."

   For each judgment, talk about what the child actually said or did that led you to this judgment.

   What did this exercise help you learn about yourself as an observer? What did you learn about the child you observed?

4. **Think about the purposes of objective observations, interpretations, and questions.**

   Turn to page 43. What do you notice about the two observation records at the top of this page?

   Observe a child this week.

   Record your observation by using the format on page 44. Take objective notes and document your interpretations and questions.

Chapter 4: Guidelines for Effective Observation

This chapter offers the following guidelines to being an effective observer:

- Observe over time.

- Watch children in varied situations.

- Keep track of what you see.

- Observe in and out of the action.

Discussion Questions

- Review the story of the daffodil patch on page 56. How can you use that story to convey the importance of observing over time to a new teacher? ... to a parent?

- What do you think about when you hear the term *classroom observation*? How many different ways can you think of to learn about a child? (See pages 55–56.)

- Why is it important to record what you observe? (See pages 61–64.)

Exercises

1. **Think about various observation strategies: stepping back, observing in the action, reflecting after the action.**

   During the week, do one or two observations using each strategy. Remember that you can gain a tremendous amount of important information by observing for 2 to 3 minutes. (See pages 62–63 for an overview of each strategy.)

   Share your observation experiences with the group.

Brainstorm ideas about the advantages and disadvantages of each of these strategies: 1) stepping back and observing, 2) observing while participating in the action, and 3) reflecting on the action after the fact and making some notes.

How can using all three strategies make you a more effective observer?

2. **Watch a child in varied situations.**

Choose a child to observe. Conduct 3 to 4 observations of the child, making sure that the child is in a different situation each time. (See pages 58–60.)

Reflect on the questions below (and on page 60) and jot down your thoughts.

- Is the child's behavior the same in all situations?

- What did you notice about behavioral changes (or the absence of change) depending on with whom the child was interacting, where the child was, and the time of day?

- In what ways was the child's behavior affected by preferences, choice, and confidence?

Share your observation experiences and reflections with the group.

What insights did you gain from this observation experience?

Chapter 5: Becoming a Skilled Observer

This chapter discusses observation as an ongoing process of asking questions and seeking information to answer those questions. The most basic questions include these:

- What do I want to find out?

- When and where should I observe to get the information I want?

- How do I record what I observe?

- How am I going to organize the information I collect?

Discussion Questions

- Think about your most recent observations. What were some of the questions you were trying to answer? (See pages 66–69.)

- Think of a child you want to get to know better. What do you want to find out about this child? How does that influence when and where you will observe?

- On page 6, a teacher says that, at the end of last year, she discovered a pile of index cards in her desk with observation notes that she never used. Do you have a similar story or know of someone who does? Why do you think this happens even though teachers know the importance of observing?

- How do you record your observations? Do you already use some of the ideas in this chapter? What other ideas do you want to try? Do you use any different methods?

- How do you organize the information you collect? Rate how well your system works for you. Use a scale of 1 to 5, where 1 means "My system works" and 5 means "I'm in danger of finding a bunch of index cards stuffed in my desk at the end of the year."

Exercises

1. **Think about the importance of wondering and asking questions.**

   Refer to the chart on pages 67–68.

   Choose a child whom you want to know better or an area in your program or classroom that you want to know more about.

   Identify questions you will try to answer during the next 2 weeks. Write them down.

   Share your questions with the group.

   Observe for 2 weeks.

   Share what you learned with the group.

   Did observing lead to any surprises? Did you learn anything you were not expecting to learn?

2. **Make observation work for you.**

   With a learning partner, discuss what works and what doesn't in the observation system you have developed and are currently using. If you don't already have a system, envision how you would like it to work.

   What new ideas do you want to apply to your observation system? If you don't currently have a system that works well for you, use the information in this chapter to plan one that will be useful.

   Try your system for 2 weeks.

   Compare notes about how things are going and revise your system as necessary to become an even more skilled observer.

Chapter 6: Using What You Learn

Chapter 6 offers stories about how observation can help you to

- Support individual children

- Respond to the group

- Balance group and individual needs

- Conduct assessments and report information about each child's development and learning

- Work together with families

Discussion Questions

- Talk with a partner about a recent experience you had observing and responding to a child. How did you respond? What had you observed that prompted your response? Was your response effective? How did you know?

- Reflecting before responding is a challenge. What are some ways to create time for reflection?

- Discuss a time when your observations led you to adapt the environment, schedule, routines, or activities. What happened?

- Review the possible responses to children that are listed on pages 103–104. Think about how your decision about how to respond to a child is based on the child's observable behavior. Share personal examples.

- Share examples of experiences where you have used these responses. What are some other ways you respond to children based on what you observe?

- Think of a time when you talked with a family member about how best to respond to a child. What happened? How did the family member's observations and ideas help you to support the child?

Exercises

1. **Wonder about, question, observe, interpret, and respond to a child's behavior.**

    Choose one of the following behaviors to discuss:
    1) choosing the same interest area each day, 2) crying,
    3) playing or working alone, or 4) repeatedly tapping
    another child's shoulder.

    Brainstorm a list of possible explanations for the behavior
    you selected.

    For each possible explanation, discuss how you might
    respond.

    What are some ways to figure out whether your
    interpretations of a child's behaviors are accurate? What
    happens if you are wrong?

2. **Reflect on some of your observations.**

    Look at two or three of the observation notes you
    collected about one child. Reflect on the following
    questions and jot down your thoughts.

    What was going on in that situation? What was the child
    experiencing?

    What does this tell me about

    -   the child as an individual

    -   the child's skills and knowledge

    -   how the child approaches learning

    How can I use this information to build a better
    relationship with this child?

    How do I use this information to extend the child's
    thinking, understanding, knowledge, and skills?

Does the child need me to step back and let her explore independently? Does the child need my assistance? If so, how much and what kind of assistance does the child need?

What can I do to sustain the child's excitement about learning and sense of competence?

As you thought about what the child did and said, did you discover something new about the child?

Share and discuss your reflections with your learning partners.

3. **Plan for a group with diverse needs.**

    Plan an activity for a small group of children.

    As you plan, think about your recent observations of these children. What do you know about their individual strengths, needs, and interests? How will the activity address the needs of individuals and, at the same time, your goals for the group?

    During or after the activity, jot down your observations.

    Reflect on individual children's experiences. How did the activity go? If you were to conduct the activity again, would you make any changes? Based on the children's responses to the activity, what would you plan next?

    Share your experiences and thoughts with your learning partners.

4. **Discuss ways to share observations with families.**

   Brainstorm a list of ways to share observations with families.

   Discuss ways to encourage parents to notice their children's development, learning, interests, and personality at home. List ways for teachers to engage families in focusing on different aspects of their children's development and learning.

   Share your ideas with your partners.

Chapter 7: Getting Started: Observing Every Day

The last chapter reminds readers of the importance of remembering the benefits of observation. It offers

- Tips for getting started

- Strategies for making observation part of your daily routine

Discussion Questions

- Tell about a time you learned something new. How did it feel? What made the situation comfortable or uncomfortable for you?

- Read and discuss the quote from a teacher on page 144. She explained, "I'm the type of person who wants to do it right. Since I'm not really sure what to do and how I'm supposed to organize my notes, I'm too nervous. I can't seem to get started." Do you feel the same way? What can you do (or advise her to do) to feel less nervous?

- How do children benefit from sharing in your process of observing and documenting their learning? (Think about the stories on pages 147–149.)

- What do you now think about the role of observation in teaching, as compared with your thoughts when you first started to read this book?

Exercises

1. **Observe with a colleague.**

   Invite a colleague to be your observation partner.

   Take turns observing or conduct joint observations. (Refer to page 145 for ideas.)

   Share your observation notes.

   Discuss similarities and differences in what you saw and documented.

2. **Jot down notes about conversations with children**

   Have a conversation with a different child each day and take notes about the conversations.

   Make a plan for following up each conversation.

3. **Reflect on your observation practices.**

   How do you feeling about the way you observe? How has it affected your teaching? How have you incorporated observation into your everyday routine?

   What new insights have you gained about observing and teaching?

In Closing ...

We hope that you found this study guide helpful. We're confident that you will come up with additional ideas as you use it. Please let us know what they are so that we can share them with others. We will appreciate your writing to us through the special section of our Web site, www.PowerOfObservation.net.

Frequently Asked Questions

In our conversations with caregivers and teachers across the country, many questions arise as teachers begin to observe regularly. Sometimes these questions get in the way of observation even as teachers acknowledge the importance of observation.

In some cases, a change in attitude about observation is required; in others, concrete suggestions can be tried. Sometimes a combination of the two is required. We hope you find some of these ideas applicable to your situation— and that they inspire you to come up with your own solutions to questions and challenges you encounter.

Q: Am I doing this right?

Many teachers let their fear of observation stop them from observing at all. And as the days, weeks, and even months pass without recording one observation, any inclination to begin observing is stifled by their feeling that they have missed so much, they will never be able to catch up. As one teacher told us:

> I don't observe because I'm not sure I'm doing it right. Then, when I think I might give it a try, I feel I am so far behind, I'll never be able to learn all I should about the kids in my room. So I don't observe, and I feel bad about it.

A: Observation is a skill that takes time to master. Even the best observers find they become better observers with practice. Asking yourself, "How can I improve my observation skills?" is much more helpful than worrying whether you are doing it right. Of course, there will be times you miss something important about a child. But what you miss pales in comparison to how much you can see if you observe regularly.

Sometimes, when we begin something new, we set unrealistic expectations for ourselves. Instead of saying, "I'd like to observe in my classroom more," most of us decide we're going to observe every day. Many add that their observations will include at least three observations of activities and three observations of children. The problem with setting such high expectations is that most often, after less than a week, we feel we've failed.

Give yourself time to integrate observation into your daily schedule. Try not to set yourself up to fail by setting unrealistic goals for how much time you'll spend observing or how many notes or matrices you'll have by the end of the week.

Allow yourself time to get comfortable with your style as an observer. Give yourself a chance to experiment with methods of recording and realize that trial and error is often the route to success.

Q: It is hard for me to step out of the action because I would rather be doing than watching. How can I develop the habit of observing regularly?
Have you ever felt this way? For many caregivers and teachers, "doing" comes naturally. The give-and-take of interacting with children is immediately rewarding. And, as you know only too well, there is always a child who needs extra attention or something else to attend to.

Some caregivers and teachers feel guilty about taking time to step back to observe. They are afraid they are not doing their job unless they are interacting directly with children. This myth is reinforced when their co-workers and supervisors who do not value observation send them withering glances.

Still others are afraid of "losing control" if they step back They fear children may "act out," or that they may lose the feel of what is going on if they are not directly involved.

A: As we discussed in chapter 4, you have options. You can observe by participating in the action and by reflecting on the action after the fact.

In a situation where you want or feel you need to step back, the decision whether to do so often boils down to two things: how you see your role and your view of observation. If you feel you are the center of everything that is going on, it is little wonder that you find it difficult to step back. On the other hand, if you see yourself as a facilitator of learning and feel that children learn from interacting with their environment, each other, other adults who may be present, and you, it is easier to believe that positive things can happen even if you are not actively involved.

And what about your view of observing? How important is it to doing your job well? As you know by now, we believe that observation is essential to teaching and assessing young children. Although situations will come up that need your immediate hands-on attention, observation is as valuable as anything else you do during the day.

It can be difficult to continue observation when a co-worker doesn't feel the same way—and even more of a challenge when a supervisor feels observation is a waste of time. Unfortunately, there is no easy way to turn someone into an observer. It is a process that often takes time. You may want to explain, "I observe in order to be able to get to know children and respond to their individual needs." It may help to share with them concrete examples of how observation has guided your response to a child. You may also want to share this page—or this entire book. In the meantime, we encourage you to stand firm and continue observation.

Here are a few suggestions to help you make "stepping out of the action" more successful:

- Remember, you can see a lot in a short amount of time.

- Discuss how to handle observation with your co-worker(s) (if you have any) beforehand. Cue your co-worker when you are ready to "step out" so the co-worker will know to focus on the whole group.

- Arrange for an extra pair of hands if there is a child or situation that will require some intense observing.

- Choose times to step back when most children are engaged.

- Let children know what you are doing and encourage them to get help from one another.

Q: I'm too busy to observe. How can I find the time?

It can be a challenge to find time to go to the bathroom or eat lunch some days, let alone to observe, even under the best of conditions. And when your class size is larger than optimum, the demands on your time are greater still. As one caregiver put it:

> If the day is crazy, you can't observe—even if you have questions.

A: There will always be difficult days. But does that mean you are not observing? Or that you may not have time to record what you see, or even think about it until things quiet down?

Because observation is a way of being with children, you observe no matter what is going on around you. If you are having trouble recording observations, ask for help. If you provide them with an easy-to-use framework, supervisors, colleagues, student teachers, and special area teachers can, for example, jot down a child's language or check off whether a child completed a puzzle. Don't let your concern that someone may end up recording observations that aren't objective or accurate prevent you from enlisting help. Remember, you can decide which notes to keep and use.

Ironically, if you are having too many crazy days, observing more often may help you identify the cause of the craziness—and give you insight about ways to regain a sense of order.

Q: How can I get my children to let me observe?

Sometimes teachers tell us that they want to observe, they have their tools ready, they start observing, and then they're interrupted by numerous requests from their students. Balancing the ongoing needs of children and your need to observe and record is a skill that requires some practice and advance planning.

A: In trying to balance meeting many needs with observation, here are several ideas that may help. Some of these apply to children of all ages; others are for a particular age group.

- **Some situations require an immediate response.**
  There will be many situations in which responding
  to children directly is more important than recording
  notes that can be jotted down later. Chances are, the
  younger the children you work with, the more often
  you will end up putting aside your notes. That's okay.
  It's the way it should be to keep children safe and
  show them they can trust you.

  With infants and toddlers, a prompt response is often
  essential. If you are jotting down a note about Jason,
  and you spot Rachita climbing on the back of the sofa
  across the room, your priority is to move quickly to
  protect her from falling. Your notes can wait.

- **Work closely with your co-workers.** Learn to cue
  each other using a few words, a look, or a gesture.
  When a co-worker catches your eye and knows, for
  example, that you are going to step out of the action
  for a few minutes to jot down some notes, she realizes
  that she will have to keep her eyes on the whole
  group—and alert you if she needs you. If you are
  the sole adult in a family child care home, consider
  asking a parent to come occasionally so you have the
  opportunity to step back.

- **Talk with children about what you are doing.** As
  children get older, you can explain what observation
  is—how you watch and listen to them to get to know
  them better. Some teachers bring this up at a class
  meeting by asking children, "How do you think I learn
  about what you do and know?" To make the point
  more concrete, you may want to ask children to tell
  you something they would like you to watch. Then,
  after you have observed, talk together about what
  you learned. Often we forget how little time it takes
  to give children explanations about what we're doing.
  Sometimes, a simple, "I'm busy observing now, I'll come
  and talk to you in a few minutes," is all that's required.

- **Arrange the environment to increase children's independence.** Creating a safe environment is the first priority so that children can be free to explore and play, and you can be free from worrying about hazards, such as electrical outlets without covers and fish tanks that can be toppled by jostling of enthusiastic "fish feeders." Diaper changing can be a time for enjoying being together when supplies are organized and easily accessible. Older toddlers can wash their own hands when they use the stepstool you've placed near the sink, and preschoolers can put their toys away more independently if the shelves are labeled with pictures showing where things go.

- **Teach children ways to function more independently.** Teaching classroom procedures and routines (how to wash and dry hands, the rules about getting a drink of water, etc.) can save time. In addition, you can teach children strategies to try to solve their own problems before approaching you for help. Teachers use many different strategies to increase their students' self-reliance. In classrooms that use the "three before me" rule, for example, students try to get their problem solved by asking three other people for help before asking the teacher. These and other strategies make a noticeable difference in the amount of time teachers have to observe. When teachers begin to encourage independence, they are often amazed by how much children can do by themselves.

Q: How can I find time to write everything down—let alone review what I have recorded?

Not having enough time comes up in every workshop we have given about observation. We hope you take away these two messages from this book: You can and do observe without recording, and recording is valuable because it gives you something to refer to later on. As one teacher told us:

> Recording takes away the pressure of trying to remember thousands of details. It also keeps them from getting all mixed up inside your head.

A: Once again, be realistic. Don't try to write everything down— especially at the beginning of the year when everything is new. We recommend you focus on being there—on observing the special details that make each child unique and on building relationships. Remember, it is unnecessary and unrealistic to think about recording something about every child or every event in the day.

As things begin to settle down, put observing and recording into your daily schedule two or three times a week. To help you find time to jot down notes during busy times, think ahead a bit when things are calm. Be clear about what you want to look for. Consider times of the day that lend themselves more easily to observation, such as small-group time and when children are playing independently. Record a word or two, a sentence, marks, or other symbols that have meaning to you on a checklist or grid.

Take the same approach to finding time to read and think about what you have recorded. You may find that a structured plan will help make reflecting on your written observations a natural part of your work. One teacher told us she set a timer for 10 minutes every Tuesday afternoon to read her notes.

> Even though I couldn't read every observation in that amount of time, I was reading more than I had been: nothing. Slowly, it got to be a habit.

Q: How can I be objective when I care so much and am so involved in the lives of these children?

Children need you to care. At the same time, they need your objectivity, something that is difficult for their families to give them. You need your objectivity to see and respond to children for who they are. Giving both your care and your objectivity requires an ongoing balancing act, which is at the core of being a professional who works with young children and families.

A: You are your own best resource in your work with children. The fact that you worry about your ability to remain impartial can give you confidence. Recognizing that you may not be objective is the first step toward becoming an effective observer. This, in turn, will help you get to know children and make decisions that best support their development and learning.

We encourage you to reread chapter 3, in which we take a look at who you are as an observer and what you bring to observation. Also, ask a colleague to come observe with you when you are concerned that your feelings might be getting in the way of seeing a child clearly. Having outside observations to compare with yours will help you gauge your objectivity and take a caring step back if necessary.

Resources

This resource list is by no means comprehensive, but it does includes those resources that have been especially helpful to us in our work as teachers and staff developers.

Bentzen, Warren R. *Seeing Young Children: A Guide to Observing and Recording Behavior* (5th ed.). Clifton Park, NY: Delmar, 2004.

This guide provides detailed information about observing and recording young children's behavior. Many different recording techniques and instruments are included.

Boehm, Ann E. and Richard A. Weinberg. *The Classroom Observer: Developing Observation Skills in Early Childhood Settings* (3rd ed.). New York: Teachers College Press, 1997.

This book offers ideas for observing and documenting children's learning in systematic and child-focused ways. The authors address the observation of environmental factors that affect learning and behavior, the importance of understanding cultural and linguistic contexts, the role of observation in the assessment process, and different types of observation.

Curtis, Deb and Margie Carter. *The Art of Awareness: How Observation Can Transform Your Teaching.* St. Paul, MN: Redleaf Press, 2000.

The Art of Awareness help teachers learn how to use observation to enhance their appreciation of children's individuality and use what they learn to support each child effectively. The book is both practical and inspirational.

Dodge, Diane Trister, Sherrie Rudick, and Kai-leé Berke. *The Creative Curriculum® for Infants, Toddlers & Twos* (2nd ed.). Washington, DC: Teaching Strategies, Inc., 2006.

This curriculum provides a comprehensive yet easy-to-use structure for planning and implementing a high-quality program for children under age 3 and their families. It also shows how caregivers and teachers use information gathered through observation to build responsive relationships with children and families.

Frank, Carolyn. *Ethnographic Eyes: A Teacher's Guide to Classroom Observation.* Portsmouth, NH: Heinemann, 1999.

Ethnographic Eyes translates ethnography (the systematic study and description of culture) into concrete methods that educators can use to understand the diverse patterns of classroom life that are not always apparent when other approaches to observation are used. Frank describes the practice of ethnography and includes detailed discussion of observation notes and case studies.

Good, Thomas L. and Jere E. Brophy. *Looking in Classrooms* (9th ed.). Boston, MA: Allyn & Bacon, 2002.

This comprehensive book helps teachers understand how to use observation in their classrooms. It also includes discussions of student motivation, classroom instruction, classroom management, and adapting instruction to the needs of individual students.

Gronlund, Gaye and Marlyn James. *Focused Observations: How to Observe Children for Assessment and Curriculum Planning*. St. Paul, MN: Redleaf Press, 2005.

Focused Observations suggests practical ways for teachers to use observation purposefully and regularly. It not only provides teachers with strategies to help them make observation an integral part of their teaching, but it also focuses on how observations can inform assessment, program planning, and conducting cases studies of individual children. A trainer's video is also available.

Howes, Carollee and Sharon Ritchie. *A Matter of Trust: Connecting Teachers and Learners in the Early Childhood Classroom*. New York, NY: Teachers College Press, 2002.

Howes and Ritchie detail the nature of the interactions between children and their teachers that account for positive learning outcomes.

Martin, Sue. *Take a Look: Observation and Portfolio Assessment in Early Childhood* (2nd.). Boston, MA: Addison-Wesley, 1999.

Take a Look provides a wide range of information aimed at helping teachers observe and assess children. It includes discussions of ways to observe development, of outcomes-based assessment, and of observing children with special needs. There is an emphasis on the skill development of individual observers.

Meisels, Samuel J., Amy L. Dombro, Dorothea B. Marsden, Donna K. Weston, and Abigail M. Jewkes. *The Ounce Scale: Standards for the Developmental Profiles*. New York, NY: Pearson Early Learning, 2003.

This volume outlines developmental expectations in all domains for children ages birth–42 months. It is one element of *The Ounce Scale*, an infant-toddler observational assessment system.

Teaching Strategies, Inc. *The Creative Curriculum® Developmental Continuum for Ages 3–5*. Washington, DC: Author, 2001.

This valid and reliable instrument helps teachers conduct authentic assessments of preschool children's development and learning by observing children during everyday activities. The goals, objectives, steps, and examples outline the typical progression of development in four domains: social/emotional, physical, cognitive, and language. The tool is linked directly with *The Creative Curriculum® for Preschool*, so teachers are able to collect information that supports positive relationships and effective program planning.

Teaching Strategies, Inc. *The Creative Curriculum® Developmental Continuum for Infants, Toddlers & Twos*. Washington, DC: Author, 2006.

This valid and reliable instrument helps teachers conduct authentic assessments of very young children's development by observing them during everyday routines and activities. The goals, objectives, steps, and examples outline the typical progression of development in four domains: social/emotional, physical, cognitive, and language. The tool is linked directly with *The Creative Curriculum® for Infants, Toddlers & Twos*, so teachers are able to collect information that supports positive relationships and effective program planning.

References

Chess, S., & Thomas, A. (1996). *Temperament: Theory and practice.* New York: Brunner/Mazel.

Clay, M. (1995). *An observation survey of early literacy achievement.* Portsmouth, NH: Heinemann.

Gardiner, J. R. (1996). *Stone fox.* New York: Trophy Pr.

Goodenough, W. (1981). *Culture, language, society.* Menlo Park, CA: Benjamin Cummings Publishing.

Howes, C., & Ritchie, S. (2002). *A matter of trust: Connecting teachers and learners in the early childhood classroom.* New York: Teachers College Press.

Lally, J. R. (Producer/Writer), Mangione P. L. (Writer), & Signer, S. (Writer). (1990). *Flexible, fearful, or feisty: The different temperaments of infants and toddlers* [Videotape]. United States: The Program for Infant/Toddler Caregivers (Developed collaboratively by the California Department of Education and WestEd).

Marzollo, J. (2003). *Soccer Sam.* New York: Random House Books for Young Readers.

Osterman, K. (2002). Students' need for belonging in a school community. *Review of Educational Research*, 70(3), 323–367.

Pianta, R. (2000). *Enhancing relationships: Between children and teachers*. Washington, DC: American Psychological Association.

Shonkoff, J. P., & Phillips, D. A. (Eds.). (2000). *From neurons to neighborhoods: The science of early childhood development*. Washington, DC: National Academy Press.

Stipek, D. (2006). Relationships matter. *Educational Leadership, 64*(1), 46–49.

Warner, G. C. (1997). *The soccer mystery*. New York: Scholastic.

Judy Jablon, M.S., is a nationally recognized educator and author with more than 30 years of experience in early childhood and primary education. Originally a teacher, Judy is grounded in theory and practice that emphasize child development, observation, critical thinking, and experiential learning. In her role as early childhood consultant, Judy provides facilitation, leadership coaching, and training to a wide range of educational institutions and agencies. She has co-authored numerous publications, most recently Teaching Strategies' new DVD, *The Creative Curriculum® for Preschool in Action*.

Amy Laura Dombro, M.S., is author of numerous articles and books for teachers and families of babies and toddlers. Former head of the Infant and Family Center at Bank Street College of Education, Amy works with national organizations and community leaders to create tools for change. This may involve "translating" information so it is engaging and easy to use, or documenting the story of a change initiative and lessons learned. She is an author of Teaching Strategies' *Caring for Infants and Toddlers*.

Margo L. Dichtelmiller, Ph.D., is Associate Professor at Eastern Michigan University where her interests include assessing young children, integrating standards in early childhood teaching, and working with diverse families. She is a developer of the Work Sampling System; an author of *The Ounce Scale* (an infant-toddler assessment) *User's Guide*; and a consultant working with Head Start programs, state-funded preschool programs, and state departments of education.

Resources for Parents

Our Program for Infants, Toddlers & Twos
A Parent's Guide
Our illustrated booklet shows parents how warm and responsive care—in child care and at home—shapes the social/emotional, physical, and cognitive development of infants, toddlers, and twos and their ability to learn. This new edition includes information about the building blocks of language and literacy, math, and science.
#CB1386, $29.50 (set of 10)

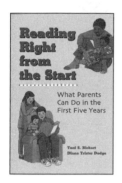

Reading Right from the Start
This book uses the everyday routines that all parents do with their children—bathing and dressing, feeding, shopping, household chores, etc.—to demonstrate how to build vocabulary, learn about conversations, and discover meaning from the written word. Instead of workbooks, special games, or other gimmicks, parents learn about the value of talking, singing, and reading to their child during common interactions every day.
#CB0045, $29.50 (set of 10)
Also available in Spanish: #CB0046, $29.50 for a set of 10

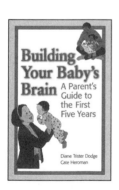

Building Your Baby's Brain
It seems that every day there are new research findings and insights into the human brain. One thing is certain—the first 5 years of life are critical for brain development. This clearly written booklet, packed full of illustrations and helpful charts, explains what scientists know about brain development and shows how a few simple things parents do every day can make a big difference.
#CB0003, $29.50 (set of 10)
Also available in Spanish: #CB0005, $29.50 for a set of 10

A Parent's Guide to Preschool
Explains how children learn while they play in a high quality preschool program and the important role parents play in helping their children succeed in school and in life.
#CB0170, $29.50 (set of 10)
Also available in Spanish: #CB0171, $29.50 (set of 10)

The Creative Curriculum® for Infants, Toddlers & Twos, 2nd edition

This comprehensive curriculum helps teachers create the very best program for children under age 3. The new edition retains its focus on building relationships, responsive care, and routines and experiences while updating the curriculum in many new ways.
#CB7996, $44.95

The Creative Curriculum® for Preschool, 4th Edition

This completely updated edition keeps its original environmentally-based approach and clearly defines the teacher's vital role in connecting content, teaching, and learning for preschool children.
#CB0019, $39.95
Also available in Spanish: #CB0155, $39.95

Building the Primary Classroom: A Complete Guide to Teaching and Learning

Provides the organizational and practical strategies primary teachers need to build great classrooms. Includes six strategies for teaching and learning: Knowing the Children You Teach, Building a Classroom Community, Establishing a Structure for the Classroom, Guiding Children's Learning, Assessing Children's Learning, and Building a Partnership with Families.
#CB0088, $32.50

DVDs and Videos

The Creative Curriculum® for Preschool in Action: This new DVD provides an in-depth examination of *The Creative Curriculum for Preschool* and shows how teachers use *The Creative Curriculum* to guide their thinking and decision making about teaching and learning.
#CB1508, $174.95, DVD

Observing Young Children: Learning to Look, Looking to Learn: This 30-minute videotape illustrates how staff can use ongoing observation to learn about each child, measure children's progress, and evaluate their program. #CB0054, $55.00, Video